Awakening
IN PURSUIT OF
THE DIVINE PARADOX

"Greetings" by Fethi Meghelli, 1993

Awakening
IN PURSUIT OF
THE DIVINE PARADOX

Gregory R. Huth

ALYSSUM

ECUMENICA PRESS, an imprint of Alyssum
Ivy League Communications Group International
Whitneyville, Connecticut

ALYSSUM

Ecumenica Press
Ivy League Communications Group International
Post Office Box 6714
Whitneyville, CT 06517-6714 USA
www.ecumenicapress.com

Library of Congress Catalog Card Number 99-073533
Huth, Gregory R.
    Awakening: In Pursuit of the Divine Paradox / by Gregory R. Huth
    Included bibliographical references and index.
    1. Religion   2. Inspiration   3. Theology   4. Self-help
ISBN 0-9669019-3-2

To the loving memory of my parents,

Raymond E. Huth
and
Mildred E. Huth

Contents

vii

Acknowledgments

This project has been so long in the making — 20 years or more, I've lost track — that I fear I will neglect thanking someone who may have read one of its many drafts, discussed a thorny issue over a beer, or delivered some point in a sermon or simple conversation that became part of my life over time and incorporated into my way of thinking. Dear colleagues, even if you're not mentioned here, thanks for your help. It's vital to note that almost everyone who has read this manuscript has not agreed with some espoused position; some readers more than others. So even as I am deeply indebted to the people that I mention here, no one of them necessarily agrees with all the concepts that are presented in this work.

Particularly strong influences came from clerical and academic friends and colleagues when they were with me in the New Haven, Conn., area including Anthony Alberg, who said he actually enjoyed reading my earliest drafts; the Rev. Robert Brusic, who introduced the concept of paradox to me at a seminal stage of project development, as well as the Rev. A. Carl Sharon, who pointed out to me the strong theme of unity-in-diversity that ran through the manuscript. Professor Emeritus Jaroslav Pelikan, a legend of Yale University history and religious studies departments, kindly recommended Charles Harper of the University of Oxford as a reader of one of my later drafts, and I am deeply grateful for Professor Harper's comments. Thanks to my pastor, the Rev. Michael Merkel, who was kind enough to offer thoughtful feedback on a semi-final draft.

I am also indebted to longtime publishing colleague and design collaborator, Susan Brown Schmidler, whose design and layout of the book and its dust cover well represent her professionalism and esthetic grace.

Finally, to my wife, Ellen McNally, for supporting me through the Wagnerian *Sturm und Drang* that accompanied the writing and rewriting of this manuscript over so many years; with hopes pinned on publisher after publisher, hearts soaring with every manuscript submission and crashing with every rejection, until finally this, the end of that long, long night with the dawn of Ecumenica Press — my deepest thanks and love.

Introduction

This book began as a series of reflections on my own spiritual life that I started back in the late 1970's and early 1980's, before commencing work on a master's degree in public health at the Yale University School of Medicine. Many philosophical questions lingered unanswered from my college days in the early 1970's, and I felt impelled to deal with them. Most of these issues, relating to heaven and hell, the relationship between faith and science, and the wide world of spirituality outside the Christian tradition, stemmed from my moving on from the fundamentalist Christianity in which I was brought up. Problem was, I no longer could rely on the simple, often inflexible approach to complex questions that the church of my youth had provided.

Flash forward now to 1986, on a Metro-North commuter train, where some of the most important aspects of this book took root. By this time I was working as a senior editor for Corporate Affairs at CBS, Inc., in New York. One of the few things that commends the two-hour commute between New Haven, Conn., and New York City is that it allows plenty of time to catch up on one's reading, and I had gotten into the habit of perusing a chapter or two of the Bible on my morning trip to work.

1

It wasn't just my Bible reading, though, that got the creative wheels turning, but another, far smaller book entitled *Zen Flesh, Zen Bones*, by Paul Reps. Having picked it up from my apartment mate's bookshelf about 10 years before, in my bachelor days, I hadn't returned it — and I must confess to my embarrassment that I have not returned it to this day! Time after time over the years I had begun to read the book, a collection of Zen *koans*, or stories of wisdom, but finding them frustrating and frankly nonsensical, each time I had given up after getting through only a few pages.

Time passed, and both my apartment mate and I got married. As my wife and I moved from apartment to apartment over the years, *Zen Flesh, Zen Bones* came with us as part of our small library. Finally, as a commuter a decade after I first "borrowed" the book, I decided that the enforced idle time of the train would provide me with the structure that I needed to get through it. I intentionally left my *New York Times* at home; either *Zen Flesh, Zen Bones*, or utter boredom would possess my time.

This approach proved successful. I was finally able to read all the way through this collection of very short stories, maddening in the enigmas that they presented. In some instances, the *koans* didn't make sense; at other times, their plots worked out in a way that was unfair to the protagonist.

All right, perhaps life was like that, too, but weren't religion and philosophy supposed to help us clarify things, to help us make sense of our everyday frustrations?

To illustrate just some of the maddening scenarios presented in the *koans*, there were tales of loyal disciples or people who wanted to become disciples who were regularly spurned by capricious spiritual masters without so much as an explanation. In one story a test of knowledge in one monastery was won not by monks who offered insightful verbal gems, but by one who stood up, tipped over a delicate glass vase with his foot, spilling its water onto the floor, and then left the room without uttering a word. This was particularly galling to me, as one who made his living by the written word.

Because of the *koans'* troubling, apparently illogical nature, I found that I could not read more than a few at one sitting; they were like sitting down to a box of the richest and most subtle chocolates — one couldn't gobble, only sample and savor. I often found myself meditating on a single one with the all the energy that I might dedicate to trying to solve an entire *Times* crossword puzzle. After a few days of engaging in this struggle with the *koans*, however, I noticed an effect that took me totally by surprise. For, despite the challenging, paradoxical nature of these stories — or as I would come to recognize, because of their use of paradox — I was left with a profound sense of peace.

Paradox. Paradox. Just what is paradox?

My dictionary defines it as "a statement that seems contradictory, unbelievable or absurd, but that may actually be true in fact." For the purposes of this book, I paraphrase this as, "an apparent contradiction that is actually true."

As for Zen *koans*, on the surface, these stories confront the reader with an apparent contradiction to common sense, fair play, or even moral values. Yet the stories are structured to do just this. They are intended to make the reader uncomfortable, not for the sake of discomfort, or to advocate injustice or immorality, but to engage the reader in a struggle with the apparent contradictions that frustrate us if we use everyday thinking, and yet if we reflect, make sense as paradoxical wisdom.

To make this leap to wisdom successfully, the reader of *koans* has to take three steps. First is to transcend, or move beyond the literal, conventional meaning of the story. From this transcendent perspective, the reader often discovers the paradox that unites or synthesizes the apparently irreconcilable ideas. And in this realization, the reader gains insight that transforms him or her in an important way, a result that Zen masters term "enlightenment."

Transcendence. Unity. Transformation.

Pay careful attention to these words. They will serve as the watchwords that guide us through our remarkable journey into paradox. They will guide us in our trek from before the birth of time and the universe to beyond their demise; from the submicroscopic beginnings of the cosmos to its farthest reaches; from the very depths of hell to the highest heaven.

I must admit that the sense of peace evoked by my struggle with *Zen Flesh, Zen Bones* was accompanied by more than mere surprise; my experience was tinged with unease, even guilt. After all, I was a committed Christian, as I still try to be today, and was frankly puzzled by the deep feeling of well-being that I was receiving from the literature of another religious tradition — the Eastern tradition, for heaven's sake. Earlier religious experiences had always been within the context of Christianity, and thus I had always attributed them to the work of the Holy Spirit.

Was it possible that the Holy Spirit was, well, ecumenical? Could God be reaching out to me through Zen, a discipline that sprang from Buddhism? Amid what I thought of then as vaguely heretical thoughts, it began to dawn on me how important paradox was to Christianity, as well.

I also began to realize just how badly we Christians ignored and undervalued paradox in our tradition. For instance, most Christians at least pay lip service to the paradoxical teaching of our one God as a Holy Trinity, comprising three co-equal Persons. But even as many churches can boast of standing room only to celebrate the birth of Christ on Christmas and his resurrection on Easter, as a rule, congregations' ranks do not swell at Pentecost, the festival of the Holy Spirit. Our worship behavior as Christians thus betrays that we do not relate to the Son and Holy Spirit as Persons that deserve equal devotion.

As for the mystery of the Trinity, from a relatively early age, I myself have struggled with a Deity who is at once one, yet also a Godhead comprising three Persons. It's an uncomfortable concept that I think most Christians accept mostly because people whom we trust implicitly have taught it to us. Without wrestling much with this apparent contradiction of Three-in-One and One-in-Three, we compartmentalize it away with other peculiar, difficult things we have been taught, such as algebraic equations and $E = mc^2$, but never have much hope of really understanding.

I think that at least part of our discomfort with paradox is a matter already mentioned, that understandably, we come to religion looking for answers that will help us define our lives, not for puzzles that will further confuse us. It's tempting to approach Christianity or any religion looking for black and white answers to such troubling questions as who we are, where we come from and where we are going. In fact, if our psychological or emotional needs depend desperately enough on our own version of black and white, we will fight, sometimes to the death, with people who have come up with different answers.

Oddly enough, we may reserve our most hostile reactions for those who have come up with virtually identical answers that they happen to express differently. By way of example, the long and bitter struggles between various Christians denominations come to mind — and sometimes within those denominations. And then there are the traditional, bitter battles that rage into the present day between Christians, Jews and Moslems.

It's my belief, however, and the premise of this book, that paradox can help us of various faiths to transcend the world of black and white and help us discover the colors of the rainbow that God has given us all to shine forth. From our transcendent perspective, we can even come to accept that beyond what the eye can see is light such as ultraviolet and infrared that affects our lives just as profoundly as does the visible spectrum. Opening our hearts and minds to such possibilities can be liberating and enlightening — and to a species that has endangered itself such as ours, perhaps even saving.

Christians should remind themselves that Jesus himself used paradox to instruct his disciples, as evidenced in several of the stories that have been handed down to us in the New Testament. Such stories as the vintner who paid his laborers the same wage regardless of their hours and the prodigal son, are known as *meshalim* in Hebrew. These stories use the same method as Zen *koan*s, posing situations with apparently unfair or illogical outcomes in an attempt to lead the reader to wisdom by discovering the overarching paradox. Interpreting these stories, with an eye to paradox, forms the backbone of this book, along with complementary discussions of the Adam and Eve story from the book of Genesis, and the enigmatic image that Jesus told of how it is easier for a camel to pass through a needle's eye than for a rich man to enter heaven.

Through these challenging little stories and images, Christians may find that entering the transcendent realm of paradox is no mere intellectual exercise, nor is it reserved for those of Eastern religions. These stories can lead us to new insights into such difficult paradoxes as:

- God, the loving, all-powerful creator who allows injustice and suffering in the world.
- Christ, the savior of the world, who also is the universal judge over heaven and hell.
- Humanity, created in God's image, which also poses the greatest threat to itself and the life of the planet.
- Hell, a realm of eternal spiritual punishment that was created — or at least allowed to exist — by a God who loves all souls in a more profound way than we could ever imagine.

What is more, this book discusses how, within the transcendent realm of paradox, we can discover how the most basic and fundamental Christian beliefs are not contradicted — but indeed are complemented — by the discoveries of science, including the latest theories about cosmic and life evolution.

Paradox may even serve as a portal through which Western religions enter into what University of Oxford theologian Keith Ward terms the Third Age of religion. In this Third Age, people of faith grow beyond the First Age, in which they use religion to enforce cultural tribalism with armed struggle. Most Christians today live in the Second Age, in which armed religious conflict is relatively rare but exclusivity remains, in that the group's own beliefs offer the rarefied status that goes along with walking the only true path to heaven. Third Age religious belief, by contrast, views all life-nurturing, compassionate religious beliefs —including its own — as complementary ways for imperfect mortals to relate to the Divine. Ultimately beyond human understanding, God offers to the faithful of different traditions revelations according to their own history, culture and scientific knowledge — offering humanity the opportunity to learn from its own diversity.

Awakening: In Pursuit of the Divine Paradox embraces the Third Age and urges the faithful to join in a worldwide, cross-cultural Third Great Awakening in which the Spirit of God renews and invigorates all people of faith within their own traditions. Across the religious spectrum from East and West, this Third Great Awakening is named after the Great Awakening movements that helped shape United States history during the seventeenth and eighteenth centuries as discussed in more detail in later chapters.

This book urges that God's servants focus their energy within the Third Great Awakening on the following principles:

- Inviting God's Spirit into our hearts so that we may live unselfish, compassionate lives. This will be reflected in more humane institutions, from the workplace to our prisons; conspicuous consumption and the hoarding of wealth will give way as we open our hearts to God's love.
- Building tolerance between religious faiths so that we may learn from, support and strengthen each other.
- Advancing respect and understanding between races, ethnic groups and nations.
- Encouraging the enlightened dialogue between faith and science so that our religious lives may complement our understanding of the universe, and that science and technology may advance with ethical wisdom and restraint.

Awakening: In Pursuit of the Divine Paradox attempts to approach these issues from a Christian perspective. It does so in the confident belief that tolerance for other religious traditions and openness to scientific discovery will not blur our identity as Christians but will actually help us to fulfill the promise of our spiritual heritage. Hopefully readers of other faith traditions — or with no particular religion at all — will be able to apply the principles outlined here to their own spiritual lives.

Transcendence. Unity. Transformation.

In these troubled, hopeful, exciting times at the turn of the millennium, let us open our hearts and minds to the watchwords of paradox. May they enlighten us and show us the way to compassion.

PART ONE
Twelve
Paradoxes

CHAPTER 1

The Paradox of Faith

Are there times when God seems particularly close to you? There are to me, sometimes in a warm moment with family or friends, or perhaps as I'm singing a favorite hymn at church. At other times I sense God's presence when I take a quiet walk in the woods or when I pray a heartfelt prayer.

At these times I transcend my everyday cares. I feel as if I'm at one with God, with myself and with the world. And in this experience in some mysterious way, I am different than I was before; I am transformed.

Transcendence. Unity. Transformation.

Already our paradoxical watchwords have come to the fore. Not all moments of reflection, though, have this transcendent effect. Having had my eyes opened by Eden's forbidden fruit, sometimes it's not enough just to know that I believe; I want to know why. I don't find this troubling, for I'm convinced that curiosity and a healthy skepticism help my faith stay alive and grow.

Given that doubt goes hand-in-hand with faith, though, and indeed that many people do not believe in God at all, you may be surprised by the idea that I am about to propose — that there is no such thing as a faithless person.

This may seem childish at first, but I assure you it's not.

At those times when I've had to decide between belief or unbelief, I've found that my choice, paradoxically, was not whether to have faith, but rather, where to place it.

Living in the technological age that we do, some of us may assume that our daily lives hum along as if we were making our decisions logically and scientifically. But this is an illusion. For unless we are researchers in the laboratory, hard at work at our well-controlled experiments, the vast majority of our decisions have little if anything to do with the scientific method.

Referring to the universe of thought processes that comprises our everyday lives, Alan Watts observes:

> If we were rigorously "scientific" in collecting information for our decisions, it would take us so long to collect the data that the time for action would have passed long before the work had been completed. So how do we know when we have enough? Does the information itself tell us that it is enough? On the contrary, we go through the motions of gathering the necessary information in a rational way, and then, just because of a hunch, or because we are tired of thinking, or because the time has come to decide, we act. . . . In other words, the "rigorously scientific" method of predicting the future can be applied only in special cases — where prompt action is not urgent, where the factors involved are largely mechanical, or in circumstances so restricted as to be trivial.

Even in the laboratory, scientists know that their findings must be couched as probabilities based on clearly defined assumptions. Even when our experiments prove something with a probability approaching 100%, we may eventually come to discover that our assumptions were so far off base that our experiment only served to underline our ignorance. In other words, inherent uncertainty even in the scientific process requires a measure of faith to accept its results.

The Paradox of Faith

Then there's the issue of the cultural lenses through which we view our world. Theologian Langdon Gilkey reminds us that all human observation, including science, will always be subjective, because human beings observe nature in the context of their own personal and cultural experience. Even the visionary Albert Einstein, whose $E = mc^2$ revolutionized our perception of the cosmos, for years refused to believe his own calculations that the universe was expanding. Before his idea was corroborated by scientific observation years later, an expanding universe just didn't make sense to Einstein, because he was part of a culture whose reality was based on faithful acceptance of Aristotle's age-old theory that the universe was static.

Hence, enmeshed in our own subjectivity, wearing the blinders of cultural assumption, we cannot claim absolute knowledge. In a sense, what we are left with is positive versus negative faith. We size up the situation before us and make our judgment according to our imperfect data in the context of our cultural and personal prejudice, finite experience, physical perceptual limits and emotional state at the time.

This is true in decisions small and large. In deciding whether to have a second cup of coffee at breakfast, or whether to believe in and follow God. No matter which faith we choose, however, whether positive or negative, we come face to face with paradox; indeed, faith and paradox are conjoined at the hip.

This is most clearly evident, perhaps, when it comes to the big picture, our basic world view. If we view the world with negative faith, we behold the paradox of this world, which presents a bleak picture indeed. For human life is a kind of cruel joke in which we emerge from oblivion into a world that has come into being either spontaneously or accidentally; humanity, in the words of biologist and philosopher Jacques Monod, "is alone in the universe's unfeeling immensity, out of which (we) emerged only by chance."

In such a universe, we experience all the challenges and joys and agonies of existence, only to return to the nothingness from which we came.

Theologian Keith Ward discusses this paradox in terms of science taking to its absurd extreme the definition of the universe as a kind of machine that runs according to the scientific laws discovered by Sir Isaac Newton. He observes that the idea of the universe as

> ...a blind, purposeless mechanism is paradoxical, to say the least; and it leaves an ultimate mystery about the existence of the universe, which Newtonian science cannot resolve. How does the universe come to be there? And how is it that conscious, inquiring, rational, purposive human beings can come to exist in a universe which is blind, purposeless and wholly random? The great irony of the Newtonian world-view is that it is a product of the highest imaginative mathematical genius which apparently denies the existence of consciousness, imagination, freedom and rationality in the cosmic machine. It is thus a profoundly alienating view, leaving human beings as aberrant mistakes in a vast impersonal and purposeless machine.

In short, negative faith and its ultimate paradox, the paradox of this world, subordinate the spirit. What is more, living according to such a world view can have a strong impact on how we approach life. For example, if we in negative faith think of ourselves as pitiful, accidental little creatures, scurrying about on our tiny planet, an anomaly of life lost in the vast, cold reaches of the cosmos, we find ourselves powerless against the social and natural forces that give birth to us and control us. According to the paradox of this world, we may actually feel a sense of obligation to ourselves to gratify our egos as best we can with the pleasures of power, wealth and sensuality during the brief, capricious spark we call a lifetime.

The cost to others of this self-indulgence? Not our concern. It's survival of the fittest, and those who die with the most toys win.

By contrast, if we are rooted in positive faith, we view our own lives — as well as those of our fellow human beings and of the earth itself — as sacred gifts. In reverence to our Creator, we live for the protection and nurture of our fellow human beings and all life.

Transcendence. Unity. Transformation.

What a wonderful, transcendent experience it is when our lives do come together — within ourselves, with others — in loving faith. (To avoid wordiness, from this point on, the word "faith," unless otherwise noted, will refer to positive faith.) Thought, feeling and belief converge. In this integration we are transformed as we awaken to life and thus feel irresistibly called to nurture it.

In faith, we liberate the spirit; we come to a transcendent view of the cosmos and ourselves not only as proceeding, but in a larger sense, becoming. As we claim our rightful place as part of the life of the universe, aging is not our enemy, for passing time does not just reflect our moving closer to death, but more importantly, our ongoing metamorphosis. We even come to accept our own physical decline and death in the context of positive transformation, for death simply culminates our metamorphosis.

What then is the paradox of faith? I believe it's the same whether our faith is of the East or the West. The struggle of the faithful is to understand how hope can be true even though it often seems to contradict our everyday experience. We of the Western tradition, for example, worship a just, all-powerful, loving God, and consider ourselves the crown of creation, yet each day in the media, and sometimes in our everyday lives, we see plenty of injustice, cruelty, pain and death. How are we to reconcile belief in God with such overwhelming evidence of the paradox of this world?

For Christians, a good starting point is to remind ourselves that the Christ himself was well aware of the world's paradox. Nevertheless, Jesus teaches that through the ongoing work of the Holy Spirit, the tiny mustard seed of faith paradoxically grows into a mature tree that is tall and strong enough to serve as a nesting place for many birds. Christ promises that if we walk in him, he can still nurture the work of the Spirit within our hearts despite the paradox of this world. Even though we live in a world that threatens to implode under the weight of its own corruption and despair — if we do not physically explode it first.

Transcendence. Unity. Transformation.

Our watchwords again come to the fore, because paradox not only challenges our faith, but liberates and fulfills our spirits. The following chapters will discuss just how this is so.

CHAPTER 2

The Paradox of the Trinity

Many paradoxes of Christian theology became codified in the third century CE in the Apostles and Nicene creeds. Some contemporary theologians feel as if the creeds have outlived their usefulness. This book will treat the creeds as still valid and useful summaries of Christian faith, but will interpret them from a Third Age vantage point.

What are among the paradoxes raised in the Apostles and Nicene creeds? To start, they tell of a God who is all-knowing and all-powerful, an eternal Spirit who is beyond all things: a *transcendent* God. Yet paradoxically, the creeds also teach that God, as the underlying force of Creation, is everywhere, ever-present in everything: an *immanent* God.

Another paradox presents itself in the Trinity. Comprising Persons called the Father, Son and Holy Spirit, the Father creates everything other than the Deity itself, and has lived forever in perfect love and harmony with the other two coequal Persons of the Trinity. Yet the three Persons aren't separate, like three technicians sitting together in the control booth of highest heaven managing Creation. As Spirit, the Trinity is very much one, a paradoxical unity-in-diversity.

19

As the second Person of God, the Son, God's holy Word, is not created by the Father, but is forever begotten of him. Pay special note to this point; it's central and we will refer to it time and again, especially in Part II of the book. In this forever changing yet forever constant relationship, Creator and Word have shared life throughout eternity. God sent the divine Word to earth as the human being Jesus Christ ("Christ" from the Greek *christos*, a translation of the Hebrew *messiah*, the anointed one of God.) Jesus came to reveal the Creator to humanity and to save us from our sins. Born of the Virgin Mary, who conceived him not by Joseph, her betrothed, but begotten within her by the Holy Spirit, Jesus Christ is the only human being ever to have lived without sin and in perfect love.

Neither this love, however, nor the power of almighty God saved Jesus from humanity's evil. The religious and political leaders of his time had him executed, apparently for blasphemy. While it's not clear what if anything that Jesus taught or did was blasphemous, Mark's Gospel implies that Jesus' teachings were becoming so popular that he represented a threat to the authority of the religious leaders of the day. The Gospel of John presents Jesus' raising Lazarus from the dead as a miracle that was considered demonic by the religious leaders of the time.

C. S. Lewis suggests that Jesus' blasphemy was his claim to have the authority to forgive sins, thus equating himself with God. Yet from the Christian point of view, if it weren't one thing that caused Jesus' unjust demise it would have been another; for his suffering and death were paradoxically the very reasons that God sent his begotten presence to us, to become an atonement, a living sacrifice, so that God might forgive our own sins through him.

Christians have puzzled over the mystery of atonement since the time of Jesus. Such an atoning sacrifice may have made intuitive sense to the earliest Jewish Christians, who were accustomed to sacrificing animals on the temple altar as offerings to God as innocent substitutes to "pay" for human sin. In fact, the New Testament reports that Jesus died during the Feast of Passover, a holiday during which Jews celebrate when they were protected against the Angel of Death by smearing the blood of a sacrificial lamb over the front door of their homes. Hence, Christians know Jesus as "the lamb of God who takes away the sin of the world."

In later chapters, *Awakening* will further discuss the Christ's rescue of the human soul, along with another paradox with which the Creeds present us, the rather startling teaching that after Jesus dies and is buried, he descends into hell, the spiritual prison of the dead. Although the sinless Jesus ventures there not to suffer further, but to preach in triumph to those who are imprisoned there, *Awakening* will suggest why the Christ would take the trouble to deliver such a message to souls whom some Christian traditions have consigned to spiritual prison for eternity.

In death, Jesus' very body proves to be a paradox, for two days after he dies, he is resurrected. He appears to his disciples in a body transformed by the power of the Holy Spirit and preaches on the earth for 40 days. According to biblical accounts, Jesus' resurrected body also displays paradoxical traits by sometimes acting like our own, requiring food and drink, while at other times behaving like a spirit, suddenly appearing in or disappearing from various locations.

Finally, in the presence of his disciples, the earthly paradox of Jesus culminates as he is accepted directly into heaven. Ascension into heaven, in apparent contradiction of the way nature works for the rest of the human race, would seem paradoxical enough by itself. Yet Christ's ascension ushers him into another paradox that is even more profound — the savior/judge paradox.

The puzzle here is that Jesus himself says in the Bible that he has come to save all people. Yet, how does this square with his consigning some of us to prison? Later chapters will attempt to deal with this conundrum as well.

If all the paradox surrounding the first two Persons of the Trinity weren't enough, the third Person presents itself as perhaps the most mysterious. The creeds describe the Holy Spirit as somehow proceeding from the Father and the Son. The Spirit's presence everywhere (omnipresence, or immanence) allows everything to exist, and is always at work to bring all Creation into a positive relationship with God. Although one can never really characterize the Spirit's enigmatic presence, I have come to understand this Person as God's divine energy at work within the Trinity, throughout Creation and in the human heart.

In fact, the Spirit's omnipresence reveals a divine attribute that is closely related to God's immanence, God as the ultimate unity. Not only does God comprise three distinct Persons who are only one God, but this Great Spirit pervades and presides over Creation, one God who is its Alpha and Omega, its beginning and its end. Such is the profound power of the divine paradox, this mysterious unity-in-diversity.

Transcendence. Unity. Transformation.

God, the ultimate transcendence, is also the ultimate presence. To open ourselves to the divine paradox, we too must transcend, and in this we become present as never before — we enter the ultimate unity. In this oneness we are ultimately transformed.

CHAPTER 3

The Divine Paradox

Nothing which implies contradiction falls under
the omnipotence of God.

Thomas Aquinas, Summa Theologica
Ia, QXXV, Article 4

If only the Trinity were the most difficult of Christian
paradoxes. As already noted, we of the Western tradition
must try to fathom a Creator who is perfect love and all-
powerful, yet who has created a world that is marred by
injustice, cruelty, pain and death.

This may make us wonder if we're really dealing with
paradox at all, or simply contradictions that betray our
beliefs to be nonsense. For example, what about the apparent contradiction of God's immanence and transcendence?
How can something be intimately present and yet utterly
detached?

Then there's the apparent contradiction of God and
time. The New Testament describes God as the Alpha and
the Omega, the first and last letters of the Greek alphabet.
This phrase is often raised in the context of the Apocalypse
— the end of the universe — with God as the End as well as
the Beginning of all things.

But the phrase "God, the Alpha and the Omega," does not simply mean that the Creator presides over both the birth of Creation and its death; Scripture does not say that God *was* the Alpha and *will be* the Omega. Rather, it says that God *is* the Alpha and the Omega; that is, *both* Alpha *and* Omega, simultaneously the beginning and the end. Such an apparent contradiction implies that God is beyond time as well as inside of it.

This is difficult stuff. Brain circuits begin to overload as we try to make sense of a Being who encompasses opposite poles, who is at once here and beyond, intimate and re-moved, the beginning and the end; a personality who participates in time and yet beyond personality views eterni-ty as detached as we might be from the tick of a wristwatch. Such is the challenge of divine unity-in-diversity.

Yet the divine paradox isn't just a tedious mind game. It's a source of peace and wisdom and insight into existence; it's an oasis of truth from which God offers drink to parched travelers on the caravan of life. Thus we segue into the first of Jesus' *meshalim* — the stories that use paradox to tease the mind into new insights.

With these tales, the storyteller's like a scientist who wants to cause a chemical reaction. To accomplish this she must, on an atomic level, induce a quantum leap — making electrons jump into a wider orbit around their home nuclei. Only, the *meshal* teller uses paradox to bring the listener into a higher way of thinking. The goal is to cause a quantum leap to a transcendent point of view, to let the listener achieve broader awareness; to awaken the listener.

Let's now turn to the story, that of the vintner who recruits day laborers for the grape harvest.

> For the kingdom of heaven is like a landowner who went out early in the morning to hire laborers for his vineyard. After agreeing with the laborers for the usual daily wage, he sent

them into his vineyard. When he went out about nine o'clock, he saw others standing idle in the marketplace; and he said to them, "You also go into the vineyard, and I will pay you whatever is right." So they went. When he went out again about noon, and about three o'clock, he did the same. And about five o'clock he went out and found others standing around; and he said to them, "Why are you standing here idle all day?" They said to him, "Because no one has hired us." He said to them, "You also go into the vineyard."

When evening came, the owner of the vineyard said to his manager, "Call the laborers and give them their pay, beginning with the last and then going to the first." When those hired about five o'clock came, each of them received the usual daily wage. Now when the first came, they thought they would receive more; but each of them also received the usual daily wage. And when they received it, they grumbled against the landowner, saying, "These last worked only one hour, and you have made them equal with us, who have borne the burden of the day and the scorching heat." But he replied to one of them, "Friend, I am doing you no wrong; did you not agree with me for the usual daily wage? Take what belongs to you and go; I choose to give to this last what I gave to you. Am I not allowed to do what I choose with what belongs to me? Or are you envious because I am generous?" *So the last will be first, and the first will be last.*

Matthew 20:1-16 (Emphasis added.)

How do we begin exploring the paradox of this story? Well, first we have to identify its apparent contradiction. That's not difficult. People who are working for just an hour or so in the relative cool of the late afternoon are getting paid the same wages as those who have labored the entire day under a scorching sun. This just doesn't make sense; it's blatantly unfair. Whatever happened to equal pay for equal work?

The answer lies in three words: Transcendence. Unity. Transformation.

As Jesus concludes the story, he leaves us a clue that this parable has nothing to do with supervising farm labor.

Christ's reference to the "first and last" — the Alpha and Omega — invokes the language of the End of Days. By so doing, Christ invites us to take that quantum leap of awareness; in this case, to jump outside of our present time perspective and view our lives from that transcendent state that occurs just beyond time. Startled, reborn into new, transformed bodies, we find ourselves in the kingdom of heaven, in the presence of God, after time has run its course.

According to this reading, the vintner is God, and the newly employed workers, people who labor in divine service. Their work day is all human history. Unemployment signifies the spiritual malaise and lack of direction that people experience if they do not actively engage in a relationship with their Creator. The vintner's ongoing search for laborers signifies that the Holy Spirit continually seeks out people to enter into such a relationship, to pursue God's "labor of love."

This parable is of particular importance if you've been looking in vain for the meaning of life. Having taken the transcendent leap in this story, our teacher Jesus provides us with a simple answer: "To pursue God's labor of love."

Note further how the toil of the workers and the vintner's recruitment continue throughout the entire day. This shows that humanity's struggle for relationship with God continues from the dawn into the dusk of history. Hence, the "wages" being dispensed at the end of the day aren't money, for we have no use for wealth after the universe ends. Rather, the gift that God confers can be received either in full or not at all — entrance into the direct, everlasting presence.

Having transcended to the timeless perspective of God's kingdom, we immediately look about for our other two watchwords, unity and transformation. We are not disappointed.

As for unity, notice the sense of equality that emerges as "the last are first and the first are last" among God's servants. We find that in heaven there is a new way of viewing one's status as compared to our worldly way, but this change turns out not be an *inversion* of status — the rich ending up poor and the poor, rich — as we might assume. Rather, we discover a *leveling* of status. In other words, the workers who show up last do not get more than their counterparts, but the same; all the laborers are treated as equals.

With this, we also encounter the final watchword, "transformation," for no matter how long they have worked throughout history, God's laborers have been transformed to *become the same* in terms of pay. As the Creator sweeps all time and energy and matter away, a kind of synthesis takes place. In the unifying presence of their Creator, God's servants are transformed; paradoxically, the first and the last are equal; Alpha and Omega do not reverse, but reveal themselves as one.

To put an image to the concept, imagine all the vineyard workers joining hands in a circle at day's end. Then have them begin dancing in a great circle. As the revelry goes on for a while, we lose track of who was the first or the last to join the circle; all have been transformed into equal parts of the larger whole.

Now we can finally realize the paradox of the matter. Even though no one is *either* first or last, in another sense everyone is *both* first *and* last. At first, these two statements may appear to contradict, but if you think about them for a moment, both are true — and there's our paradox.

This feisty, ragtag collection of servants that the Creator has gathered from throughout history has become a unified whole in the circle dance of eternal life — transformed in reflection of the unity-in-diversity of the divine paradox.

The Paradox of Love

In the last chapter, we read one of Christ's *meshalim* as a way to transcend the point of view of our transient, fragmented world and reflect on God's paradoxical unity-in-diversity. Chapter Four will continue on this transcendent plain to consider another divine attribute: love. For it is through love that the Spirit invites us into the divine paradox.

A classic debate poses the question of whether it is God that changes over time, or just our perception of God. On one hand, there is little doubt that the latter is true. One need simply page through Jaroslav Pelikan's *Jesus Through the Centuries* or Paula Fredriksen's *From Jesus to the Christ*, to discover how Christians' perception of their spiritual master has adapted through the ages — and sometimes from decade to decade — as cultural and social environments have changed and our understanding of the universe has evolved.

As for the question of whether God changes, again we are confronted with a paradox. For the Bible tells us that God, forever one and unchanging, is love. But love is an ever-changing relationship. This is not just double-talk, as the unfolding discussion hopefully will reveal.

It's been difficult to write about love for some time now, because of the sheer overexposure of the word. We may love summer vacation or turn to Love and Sex Anonymous to help us curb our passions. This book, however, refers to love in the sense of caring for another with an open, vulnerable heart, as revealed by kindness, compassion and self-sacrifice.

Love is ever-changing because it's a phenomenon of relationship. Love cannot exist in a vacuum. It involves a being and something outside of itself, and here we can expand our meaning to include love for an object or ideal.

Moreover, to the extent that we are self-aware and consider the different parts of our own personality, we also relate to ourselves. Is this a reflection of our being created in God's image? Perhaps. For God's dynamic self is implied in the eternal begetting of the Son by the Father through the Holy Spirit and the eternal emergence of the Spirit from Creator and Word. Hence God, who is one, also has a relationship with — and within — the divine Self.

Our own self-relationship, that most personal of interactions, affects our everyday lives in a central way. A healthy self-relationship helps us to overcome the challenges, crises and tragedies that inevitably come our way. And as social beings, the quality of self-relationship goes beyond our own lives to affect others and ultimately, the world. We are each the butterfly whose flutter can stir a storm a continent away.

It takes my breath away to consider what the world would be like if each person were able to love him or herself in the healthiest sense of the word. I would settle for most of us simply feeling enough at peace with ourselves that we would nurture rather than destroy. Once we stop gnawing away at ourselves with self-doubt and self-loathing, perhaps the compulsion to manipulate and undercut one other will simply go away.

CHAPTER 4

The Paradox of Love

I would wager that most mental health professionals, whether prison psychologist or Park Avenue psychiatrist, spend the lion's share of their professional time trying to imbue some semblance of healthy self-love in their clients. Establishing self-love often represents the breakthrough — a kind of awakening — in which the patient transcends the limitations, the self- or externally imposed emotional barriers to happiness and inner peace; in this transformation, counseling has its healing effect.

Transcendence. Unity. Transformation.

We transcend our old, fragmented selves. Our personalities become one, the integrated, healthy whole that God creates us to be. And in this unity we are transformed in our Creator's image of loving self-relationship and compassion for others.

Many will disagree, but I don't think that we can be healthy, integrated individuals in the most profound sense of the word without an honest, open, intentional relationship with God. Many Christians hope that they already have such a relationship, but we all know how easy it is to become self-deceived about such things. How can we tell if our commitment to God is true? A loving approach to life may be the best evidence.

It should come as no surprise, though, that a relationship with a paradoxical divine Providence might have its own paradoxes. For example, God can be reflected even in people who would not think of themselves as particularly religious. Conversely, some who profess to be — and who may actually believe they are — dedicating their lives to God are simply deceiving themselves, according to the Apostle Paul, in his famous passage about the gifts of the Spirit:

> If I speak in the tongues of mortals and of angels, but have not love, I am a noisy gong or a clanging cymbal. And if I have

prophetic powers, and understand all mysteries and all knowledge, and if I have all faith so as to remove mountains, but do not have love, I am nothing. If I give away all my possessions, and if I hand over my body so that I may boast but do not have love, I gain nothing . . . And now faith, hope, love abide, these three; and the greatest of these is love.

I Corinthians 13 (1-3, 13)

We may better understand the very basic influence of love on our personal and spiritual development if we view this divine gift in the context of God as the Ultimate Being. Note the following progression:

1. Love as a divine attribute is not only positive, but also has an absolute or ultimate quality.
2. Because love involves relationship, it is dynamic.
3. Hence, love is the ultimate positive dynamic.

It follows that love cannot help but be creative. Hence, because God is love, we know the first Person of the Trinity as the Creator. And given that love is an irrepressible, positive dynamic, let's now take a look at how this force manifests itself in our world — God's creation — and can make an important difference in the way we — also God's creation — lead our daily lives.

Transcendence. Unity. Transformation.

Love, the divine creative force, helps us to transcend the barriers that keep us from completeness, either as individuals or as humanity. With love, we become one with God, ourselves, and with other people. And in this unity, we discover ourselves as our Creator's image and open ourselves to God's infinite, creative horizons.

The Paradox of Quantity

My heart is moved by all I cannot save;
so much has been destroyed
I have to cast my lot with those
who age after age, perversely,
with no extraordinary power,
reconstitute the world.

Abraham Joshua Heschel

How does our perception of the world change when we make the transcendent, quantum leap and embrace the love of God? On one hand, hope is reborn. No matter what our circumstances, we cannot help but feel centered and secure in the care of our Creator.

On the other hand, we neither deny the tragic nature of human life nor ignore its sin or suffering. Rather, we accept challenge and suffering as part of life, and assured of God's love for us and the world, do our best to share our love with those in need.

So, on balance, faith and hope and trust in God afford us a positive view of the cosmos and our place in it, and even leave open the door to joy. To readers who may feel ground down by personal tragedies, by the continual destructiveness of humanity, or even by their own individual sins, such a view may seem like sheer naiveté. I do not believe it is, though.

For faith in God and love for one another do not assume that humanity will necessarily save itself or the earth. As conscious beings, we remain free to build cathedrals or concentration camps. It remains an open question as to whether we will continue on our present, destructive path or decide to accept the Spirit's invitation to become more nurturing to ourselves and to the life of the planet.

I do believe, however, that the human race has the potential to embrace life deeply, profoundly, spiritually. Admittedly, this may be a leap of faith. Yet if we must leap — and we must — then let us do so in the direction of hope rather than of despair. I choose hope because of the very call to life that we have been discussing, hope engendered by a God who is incessantly creating, and by extension creating each of us as well.

To explain what I mean by this rather startling assertion — I doubt that many readers will necessarily sense the creative hand of God upon them as they read these words — let's continue our discussion of God's loving creativity in the context of another divine attribute, namely immanence. Since God is everywhere and is creating incessantly, it must be that everything — ourselves included — is in the process of being created. Looking around for evidence to support this sweeping belief, we turn to the evolution of the vast universe and of life on earth.

Scientists currently believe that our universe sprang forth about 12 billion years ago from some primal iota measuring smaller than the nucleus of an atom. In other words, the matter that comprises our bodies was once compacted with the rest of the universe as a kind of subatomic fetus. From this the baby universe was born in a cataclysm called

The Paradox of Quantity

the Big Bang, the strongest explosion the universe will ever see. The Big Bang dispersed a kind of superheated plasma from which everything in the universe has evolved.

Most of the universe's visible matter formed the billions of galaxies each comprising further billions of stars, including our own solar system and planet. The earth and its solar system probably began about five billion years ago, congealed from the dust of ancient exploded stars. After about four billion years of life evolution on earth, species *Homo sapiens* made its debut.

When we compare the grandeur of the cosmos, the wonder of life on earth and the subtlety of DNA and the human brain to the subatomic mote from which the universe sprang, we are tempted to jump to the conclusion that yes, it's obvious that we and the cosmos reflect the ongoing work of a conscious, genius creator who deserves no less a name than God.

But not so quickly, warns theologian Karl Schmitz-Moormann in his book, *Theology of Creation in an Evolutionary World.*

Professor Schmitz-Moormann points out that if the loving personality of the Creator is supposed to be reflected in his handiwork the universe, then God must have an odd way of expressing love. Part of the problem as Jacques Monod reminded us in Chapter One, is that the universe by and large is not a warm and fuzzy place.

To begin with, the visible material of the cosmos accounts only about two percent of the mass of the universe. The other mass comes from "dark matter," so named because scientists can measure its effects, but have not yet observed it directly. Next, we must reconcile our pride at being Creation's culmination with the fact that statistically speaking, humankind is quite literally insignificant! Schmitz-Moormann shows this using a wide range of quantitative measures beginning on a cosmic scale and ending with life on earth.

Tighten your seat belt, dear fellow crown of creation, for Professor Schmitz-Moormann is about to take our egos on a bumpy ride. To wit, he points out that:

- As compared to the volume of background radiation left over from the Big Bang, the amount of matter that has evolved in the universe is statistically insignificant.
- As compared to the elements of hydrogen and helium that make up the stars, the rest of the universe's atoms and molecules are statistically insignificant.
- As compared to the atoms and molecules that could combine to create life, the number that actually do is statistically insignificant.
- As compared to the volume of bacteria, the presence of vertebrate life, including human beings, is insignificant.

From one point of view, such a universe would seem to present overwhelming evidence of what we have been discussing as the paradox of this world. For in terms of quantity, organic matter, the stuff that we are made of, appears to be a cosmic glitch. And even for life on earth, the vertebrates, including the proud race of humanity, statistically represent little more than the fruits of odd random genetic mutation.

However sobered we may feel when confronted with such facts, however, Christians may take such information in stride, as the Law of the cosmos, knowledge that humbles us and puts us in our place. Gratefully, Professor Schmitz-Moormann also provides an interpretation of these data that we could call the Gospel of the cosmos — wisdom that elevates us with the good news of God's grace. In effect, he turns the paradox of this world on its head by viewing the same data from the hopeful perspective of the divine paradox.

To sum up in the words of Professor Schmitz-Moorman:

> Whereever we see something new appear of the stage of evolution in the universe, it represents a statistically insignificant amount as compared to the realm out of which it arose.

Hence,

> If quantity is accepted as the parameter to measure the orientation of evolution or its lack of orientation, one arrives at the paradoxical statement that evolution is a negligible phenomenon.

Finally,

> To make statements about the orientation of evolution based purely on quantity leads to an erroneous understanding of the evolving reality. It is the quantitative fallacy.

Schmitz-Moormann argues that if quantity were paramount in our philosophical view, then in contemplating the universe, we should spend all of our energy pondering background radiation. And when we muse on the meaning of life, we would have to limit our discussion largely to issues of bacteria. Thus we have encountered the absurdity of quantity.

What is more, a purely quantitative view could not account for the fact that the entire universe, from beginning to end, no matter how old; from edge to edge, no matter how wide, can be contained within the imagination of a single human mind, dear reader, including yours and mine. So Walt Whitman was right; we do have universes within us.

Thus we discover the paradox of quantity.

CHAPTER 6

The Paradox of Evolution

Paradox having superseded both the fallacy and the absurdity of quantity, we can begin to consider the idea that in our own little corner of the cosmos, the relatively recent evolution of *Homo sapiens* has real meaning in the saga of Creation. People who accept Jesus' teachings of a resurrection and life after death tend not to be surprised that that for human beings, at least, life indeed has meaning. For two millennia Christians have believed that human life is neither accidental nor created for its own sake; rather, that it exists for a reason: so that through God's grace, our temporal, organic nature may become everlasting spiritual presence with God.

In *Mere Christianity*, C. S. Lewis refers to this transformation as a "kind of evolution." But if literal evolution is truly God's creative process at work, could it be that God is fashioning the universe at least in part to evolve eternally conscious life? Could the universe be a kind of crucible or incubator that God uses to build an everlasting, living dominion?

Consider the breathtaking variety and complexity displayed within the universe of life on earth. If such developments reflect the power and genius of a cosmic Creator, then is it so difficult to conceive that the primal, subatomic point issuing forth when the cosmos begins could culminate with consciousness being issued into eternal awareness when the universe ends? Theologically, this suggests a kind of theory of intentional evolution.

Namely:

1. God is love.
2. Love is an ever-creative dynamic.
3. All things come from God, and God is in all things; hence,
4. All things reflect God's continual process of creation.

In short, despite the vastness of the universe and humanity's humble place within it, we can indeed view the evolution of the universe, its matter, energy and life, as part of a continuum that reveals the ongoing handiwork of our irrepressible Creator.

Thus it would be that through cosmic and life evolution and the development of consciousness, the universe literally awakens to its Creator. Thus the struggle for dignity, freedom and eternal life by any one human being would play a crucial role in the drama of cosmic awakening. And thus no one's existence — not even of the least among us — would be marginal or inconsequential in the great scheme of things.

All this sounds very grand and of great consequence. But even if this view of the universe happens to be true, does it have anything to do with the way we live our lives from day to day? Yes, very much so.

For if the pursuit of spiritual fulfillment is indeed the very engine of our being, then to acknowledge and embrace this quest would be to put ourselves in harmony with life and all Creation. By contrast, to deny or simply not recognize the quest would lead us to pursue it in other, misdirected ways, ranging from the merely less fulfilling all the way to the dangerously destructive.

We can find a relatively benign example of the quest slightly misdirected if we turn to a social movement in Western culture in the nineteenth century. Foreshadowing the present age in the developed world, especially parts of Western Europe, in which belief God is increasingly passé, many nineteenth-century people began to worship nature instead. In other words, in acknowledging Creation as God, people forsook God as Creator.

Art historian Kenneth Clark describes the psychology of this movement as:

> Total immersion: this is the ultimate reason why the love of
> nature has been for so long accepted as a religion. It is a
> means by which we can lose our identity in the whole and gain
> thereby a more intense consciousness of being.

One might be tempted to think that the above passage echoes our watchwords of transcendence, unity, transformation. One transcends individual identity, becomes one with the whole of nature, and in the process is transformed in consciousness. I would agree, except for the important issue raised by the key phrase, "... lose our identity in the whole."

It's important to distinguish between transcending one's self in God and losing one's identity in another created entity. Speaking from personal experience, in every instance when people have in some fashion asked me to "give up my identity," or "disengage my mind," with regard to whatever the cause, my warning flags go up. During the turbulent late 1960s and early 1970s while an undergraduate at Yale, I saw many people exploited by religious or political cults and other causes demanding surrender of one's mind and will.

Twelve Paradoxes

From the authoritarian shadows of cult mentality we can easily find our way down into the darkest catacombs where the quest for spiritual fulfillment has been misdirected. Visions of torch light parades in Nazi Nuremberg come to mind, dark tales of the Soviet gulag, stark photographs of the skulls piled high in the Cambodian killing fields. No matter how supposedly noble the cause, the sacrifice of one's identity — and individual conscience — leaves us liable to committing our most grievous acts of inhumanity.

How does surrendering one's will to earthly authority contrast with transcending the self in the service of God? Again I turn to C.S. Lewis to help explain. Lewis comments on life after death, but his comments apply just as well to spiritual growth in this life:

> . . . some people think that after this life, or perhaps after several lives, human souls will be "absorbed" into God. But . . . human souls can be taken into the life of God and yet remain themselves — in fact, be very much more themselves than they were before.

Lewis sets before us an apparent contradiction. On one hand, in our awakening, we get "absorbed" into God. On the other hand, in the process, we fulfill our own individuality. How can this be?

Transcendence. Unity. Transformation.

Transcending one's own narrow ego interests to become one with the life of Christ is a process of spiritual awakening in which we grow ever further into the compassion, empathy and love for which God creates us. This awakening is a continuous, lifelong discipline in which we answer the Spirit's call to make our own will consonant with God's. And in the process, we are transformed.

During this transformation, we may find ourselves fighting against our own urges to control or harm others, or hoard wealth, or engage in sex that is wanton, exploitative or adulterous. We may also feel called to take action — in extreme circumstances to sacrifice our very lives in order to do what is right. When we obey the call of conscience, we express our true self, the person that God is creating us to be.

Transcendence. Unity. Transformation.

Our life in God is a disciplined process of transcending our self-serving ways and becoming one with our Creator. This culminates when our biological life ends, and in our final transformation we make the ultimate quantum leap, becoming reunited with the infinite, eternal Self who has created us. In this, we truly discover who we are, for in ultimate transcendence, we become spiritually whole and fulfilled and mature. Our lives come full circle.

In God's image, alpha and omega are one.

The Paradox of
the Prodigal Son

Last chapter we examined individual spiritual awakening as a process that complements the evolution of the universe and life on earth. But this discussion did not touch on the difficult question of why human life — especially if a process of being born into God — is so often frightening and painful and even fraught with danger. Indeed, if humanity's role in cosmic evolution reflects God's creation of eternal, loving consciousness, then why must loneliness and emotional agony and physical pain and death be part of the bargain? And why must we human beings often be so selfish and cruel?

This restates the question of why God, who is perfect and loving and good, should author a Creation which from humanity's point of view is anything but perfect. Even if we perceive our natural environment on earth with its wondrous balance of life to be a kind of perfection, we are left with the vexing question of humanity's — and our own individual — evil. Humanity today — supposed crown of creation — is the only species that seems out of synch with nature to the point of threatening worldwide ecological collapse.

In his book, *Life in the Balance: Humanity and the Biodiversity Crisis*, Niles Eldredge, a curator at the American Museum of Natural History, documents how humanity has plunged the earth into its sixth great extinction of diverse species, the fifth great extinction having killed off the dinosaurs.

As I originally was writing these words, 700,000 acres of rain forest were ablaze, out of control, in Mexico. Some scientists had given the passing year of 1998 the apocalyptic name, "The Year the World Caught Fire," because of conflagrations that had caused catastrophic damage to rain forests in Brazil and Indonesia, as well. Ecologists blamed the fires on a combination of thoughtless land development, slash and burn agriculture, drought associated with El Niño and human disruption of rain forest ecosystems. Concerns about global warming arise as scientists announce that 1999 was the warmest year on record.

Meanwhile, ecologists say that human activities threaten fully one in eight plant species on the earth with extinction; in the United States, the figure is a shocking one in three species. Five hundred species have already vanished in the U.S.; at least 700 are endangered or threatened, and 9,000 are at risk of extinction. If we are putting this much stress on our environment with a current world population of approximately 6 billion people, what will it be like in 50 years, when the human population is estimated to eclipse 9 billion?

Our lack of stewardship for the earth is compounded by our sins against each other. Need we be reminded of our potential for cruelty from the nearly unceasing war and genocide of the passing century? And of the growing disparity between the struggling have-nots and a small "strato-class" of individuals that controls an ever-increasing share of the world's wealth?

The Paradox of the Prodigal Son

We take a sober look at ourselves and wonder how a perfect God could create such beings, who, despite our potential for love and nurture and good will, paradoxically can be so greedy and spread so much grief and death. Even if God insists on creating such cruel creatures as ourselves, why not like a good parent intervene directly and control us before we commit barbarity against each other and destroy the natural life around us?

We are making a value judgment here, that our destructive behavior is evil, whereas the destructive forces of nature, say, a tornado, or a crashing meteorite, or even a killer virus, are not. After all, people can choose between nurturing life or destroying it, while these other forces simply obey laws of physics or biology. Hence, when we consider why God allows us to act evilly, we must examine the issue of free will.

These are difficult issues. Scripture does not even mention the term "free will," to my knowledge. And biblical tradition is at best sketchy regarding the origins of evil.

At least with regard to evil, from the book of Genesis to that of Revelation, there are repeated references to Satan as the source of temptation, suffering and sin. Still, the dark angel presents a murky figure in both testaments. Satan appears allegorically as a snake in the Adam and Eve story. In the synoptic New Testament gospels (Matthew 4:1; Mark 1:12; Luke 4:1), a nondescript Satan makes an appearance to tempt Christ; Matthew and Luke tell of Jesus facing devilish temptations of worldly power and pleasure.

During his trial before Pilate, Jesus ecstatically declares that he sees "Satan being cast from heaven." This implies that Satan is a fallen angel. Yet Christ also calls Peter "Satan" when this rock of the Church tries to talk Jesus out of facing the passion and death to which God was calling him.

So which Satan is it? External force, the dark angel stir-

ring up temptation in this life and gloating over his catch of
fallen souls in the next? Or intrinsic shadow, our personal
demon, the evil potential of every human spirit?

Must it be either or? Perhaps paradox applies to the
dark side of spirituality as well as to the light, with Satan a
demonic parody of divine unity-in-diversity. To explore this
question further, we turn to another of Christ's *meshalim*, a
paradoxical parable of falling and redemption known as
"The Prodigal Son."

> There was a man who had two sons. The younger of them
> said to his father, "Father, give me the share of the property
> that will belong to me." So he divided his property between
> them. A few days later the younger son gathered all he had
> and traveled to a distant country, and there he squandered his
> property in dissolute living. When he had spent everything, a
> severe famine took place throughout that country, and he
> began to be in need. So he went and hired himself out to one
> of the citizens of that country, who sent him to his fields to
> feed the pigs. He would have gladly filled himself with the
> pods that the pigs were eating; and no one gave him anything.
> But when he came to himself he said, "How many of my
> father's hired hands have bread enough and to spare, but here I
> am dying of hunger! I will get up and go to my father, and I
> will say to him, 'Father, I have sinned, against heaven and
> before you; I am no longer worthy to be called your son; treat
> me like one of your hired hands.'" So he set off and went to his
> father. But while he was still far off, his father saw him and
> was filled with compassion; he ran and put his arms around
> him and kissed him. Then the son said to him, "Father, I have
> sinned, against heaven and before you; I am no longer worthy
> to be called you son." But the father said to his slaves,
> "Quickly, bring out a robe — the best one — and put it on
> him; put a ring on his finger and sandals on his feet. And get
> the fatted calf and kill it, and let us eat and celebrate; for this
> son of mine was dead and is alive again; he was lost and is
> found!" And they began to celebrate.

The Paradox of the Prodigal Son

Now, his elder son was in the field; and when he came and
approached the house, he heard music and dancing. He called
one of the slaves and asked what was going on. He replied,
"Your brother has come home, and your father has killed the
fatted calf because he has him back safe and sound." Then he
became angry and refused to go in. His father came out and
began to plead with him. But he answered his father, "Listen!
For all these years I have been working like a slave for you, and
I have never disobeyed your command; yet you have never
given me even a young goat so that I might celebrate with my
friends. But when this son of yours came back, who has
devoured your property with prostitutes, you killed the fatted
calf for him!" Then the father said to him, "Son, you are
always with me, and all that is mine is yours. But we had to
celebrate and rejoice because this brother of yours was dead
and has come to life; he was lost and has been found."

Luke 15:11-32

Just as with the story of the vintner and the hired
hands, Jesus piques our sense of fairness by presenting us
with an apparent contradiction. This time it seems as if the
obedient, older brother has been unfairly treated. Why
should the father reward his younger son, who displayed
such immorality, disrespect and waste, and then simply take
his older, obedient child for granted?

Just as with the story of the vintner and the laborers,
though, Jesus calls us to transcend, to redirect our righteous
indignation into a search for paradoxical wisdom. This
story's characters correspond in some ways to those in the
vintner's tale, with the figure of wealth and authority, the
benevolent father, representing God, and his sons playing
the role of ourselves, God's children.

According to this interpretation of the story, we as
God's children — at home at the family house, living in close
relationship with our divine parent — find ourselves ful-

filled, safe, loved and living purposeful lives. Once we turn our back on our relationship with God, however, we like the prodigal son very quickly find ourselves steeped in danger, dying in a world of drought and famine. In the thirst, hunger, and isolation of our spiritual poverty, the comfort of worldly pleasures deserts us.

Once we reach this realization, though, we open the door to wisdom. Just what wisdom does the prodigal son share with us? That to live disobediently is death and to live prudently is life?

Well, yes, to start. We might even feel satisfied with that obvious lesson were it not for the sullen presence of the faithful, older brother, who is not feeling very happy despite of his virtue. He's feeling cheated, and from our worldly perspective, rightly so. But from the moment we transcend this point of view, the taken-for-granted brother helps to teach us a profound lesson about the paradox of free will and love.

From our transcendent vantage point, let's first consider the generosity that the father grants to both his sons. Although this powerful figure presumably is able to exercise considerable control over his children's behavior, out of love, he does not. Both heirs are apparently free to leave the estate and spend their inheritance as they choose, wisely or not.

This is key, because without such freedom love isn't possible. Authors such as Archibald MacLeish and C.S. Lewis provide some insightful commentary on the tie between free will and love. They point out that God grants free will to us as spiritual beings — limiting divine power over us — so that we may experience love to the fullest, and thus achieve our greatest fulfillment of being. Such fulfillment is possible only when created beings have a choice as to whether they will reciprocate God's love.

If spiritual life were created without free will, then we could not call it "being" at all. It would be the existence of automatons, conscious robots, and our Creator would be a petty despot of mindless machines instead of the loving God of living beings. Thus, for the sake of providing humanity the chance to be fulfilled in love, God grants us the freedom to choose.

Even as God allows us to disobey, though, the Lord does not let our evil go unchallenged. God, who hates evil, will never cede the cosmic argument against it whether to mortal or angel. How God responds to his fallen children, though, speaks volumes about our Creator as a loving parent.

For God neither wipes us out of existence nor punishes us by taking away our freedom. Rather, God gives us the power of mind and heart so that we may come to realize the consequences of our choices. If we are wise, we come to learn that to cut ourselves off from divine relationship means condemning ourselves to self-defeat, self-punishment — a kind of self-imprisonment in a world of spiritual hunger and thirst. In our alienation we may even bring our own species to extinction. By contrast, to return to divine relationship means fulfillment.

In this we revisit another theme of the divine paradox: the tension between God as judge and God as savior. On one hand, God the judge, as perfect goodness, must hate the evil created beings do. On the other hand, this terrifying news is counterbalanced by the good news that God our savior offers us an escape from judgment.

We can begin to comprehend God as our salvation when we realize that every being, whether good or evil, exists only because the Spirit of God is present within it. When we consider that our Creator is not only ultimate love, but ultimate presence as well, we are led to conclude that God must be the soul of empathy. Thus, God shares every experience of his creations, from the peak of their joy to the depth of their pain and despair.

Because God's love is so great and divine empathy so complete, I cannot believe that the Creator can bear to have any created being suffer endlessly. As the crucified Christ teaches us, God literally does feel our pain. Thus, the righteous judge is also a merciful redeemer who wishes to rescue God's children from the emotional and psychological and spiritual pain that they bring on themselves and others.

God's mercy has important implications for our theology of awakening Creation, as revealed by this interpretation of the prodigal son story. So does the traditional Christian theme of death and resurrection. To continue this discussion, we turn to the story at the point where the prodigal son betrays his father's trust.

This young man shows all the hallmarks of a spoiled rich kid. Having led a sheltered life that protected him from true responsibility, the younger son lives a profligate lifestyle the moment he is on his own. In doing so, he in effect "dies" to everything his parent hoped him to be, a fact that the young man comes to regret when he finds himself literally dying of starvation in a foreign land.

Transcendence. Unity. Transformation.

Humbled to the point of mortification, the prodigal son transcends his wayward life by returning to the father's house in humility. In this family reunion, the merciful father welcomes him back and actually holds a celebration in his honor. The prodigal son has been transformed through a process of bitter experience, remorse, repentance and finally, wisdom.

All this is well and good for the younger son, and even for the father. But what about the justice that has eluded the older, obedient son? In his case, we literally are confronted with the paradox of the last being first and the first last. His little brother, the last son whether in terms of birth order, traditional status or family loyalty, gets celebrated as if he were the first. Adding insult to injury, the true first son is asked to attend a feast in which his wasteful sib is the honored guest.

But now let us transcend the apparent contradiction of sinfulness celebrated and loyalty left unfeted.

For just as under the paradoxical sun that shone down on the vineyard workers, reward for the two brothers does not come as a finite, worldly estate or a transient feast. Rather, in this heavenly household, the father's true reward is eternal life and total fulfillment. Hence, the older son already shares fully in all that his father can give; he has nothing more to gain. Moreover, he loses nothing by celebrating his brother's return.

What is more, paradoxically, the once immature younger son actually seems to have *needed* to leave the security of his father's mansion to discover just what riches he had left behind. Whereas the older brother already seems mature enough to appreciate the gifts that he already had. The only way for the prodigal son to gain such maturity is to use his freedom to stretch his wings — and fall.

Thus, the prodigal son's story implies that if created beings are to realize their unity with God in the most profound way and freely submit themselves to it — then some measure of falling away *may be necessary* for them, so as to learn the painful consequences. Through this process of transformation from naiveté to experience, ignorance to wisdom, prodigal children may most profoundly realize the power of divine love and come to know the value of living in harmony with their Creator.

In other words, we not only affirm the old saw: "If there were no devil, we would have to invent one . . . " but also add, perhaps shockingly: ". . . for the sake of our own fulfillment." Yet if this paradox is so, are we left to conclude that our own destructiveness is somehow positive? Has God made us and turned us loose simply that we may destroy ourselves and our world — and thus in some perverse way find fulfillment?

The answer is that no, self-destruction is not God's will for us. Neither is our destruction of the earth, of which God has entrusted us as stewards. Indeed, we prodigal children have already wreaked enough havoc among ourselves and squandered plenty enough of our natural inheritance to understand the consequences of our present course. It is now our free choice either to wane in wantonness or wax in wisdom.

Which way shall we choose?

The Paradox of Transformation

O ur meditation on the prodigal son reflected on Creation — both as product and process — and mused on how evil could have crept into the handiwork of a perfect God. More specifically, we began to consider evil and its embodiment, the murky figure of Satan. Departing from the traditional view of evil as the corrupter of a once-ideal Creation, we discussed evil as more like a byproduct, a kind of spiritual pollution, that occurs during the creation of a free, conscious mind.

To further delve into the issue of evil, we can also use the analogy of light and darkness. In the Western tradition, God not only is love, but light, while Satan is the prince of darkness. We view Satan not as God's opposite, which would imply parity, but as a shadow of alienation that exists only because of God's light.

Our discussion of the prodigal son concluded that some alienation from God, hopefully temporary, appears to be necessary in the creation of conscious being. "Evil" is the inevitable outcome of separation from God, for out of alienation's darkness fly the cruelest and most destructive thoughts, words and deeds. Hence, in the ongoing saga of our own creation, each conscious mind must come to terms with the interaction of progress and stumbling, light and shadow, good and evil that swirls tempest-like within each of us.

Thus having thrown down the gauntlet by using such judgmental words as "evil" and "good," let's finally define these terms specifically. Our frame of reference is what we have surmised to be the reason that God is creating us: to enter everlasting, transcendent life with our Creator. Hence, anything that enhances life — both in this largest sense and along the continuum of biological life — is good. Anything that works against life is evil.

We as individuals progress spiritually, then, when we move away from destroying life and toward enhancing it. Similarly, we as a society judge ourselves on whether we nurture life or weaken and destroy it. Somehow it seems that when we make progress enhancing life in one way or another, whether as individuals or as a group, we simultaneously slip in other ways. In the parlance of light and darkness, no matter how close to the light we may hope to journey, as long as we are being created, the shadow remains with us.

Or to be succinct, everyone's a sinner.

Given the uncomfortable proposition, though, that evil may actually be a necessary part of our creation, are we then exonerated of responsibility for doing wrong? The tempting argument goes something like this: "After all, if evil is required, then when we act badly, we're just doing what's necessary. Ergo, there's no such thing as moral responsibility."

Any such attempt to wiggle out of responsibility fails, though, for a simple reason. As conscious beings with free will, when given the choice between doing what is right or not, we often consciously choose the latter. In short, we're chronic sinners, eternal souls who are responsible for our acts.

This raises the aspect of Christianity that is the most feared, namely, that sin brings divine judgment. While we may be eager for war criminals or mass murderers — or even those we consider to be our personal tormentors — to get their just desserts, the thought of us paying for our own sins is nowhere as appealing. Nevertheless, when any one of us compares our own hearts against the purity of the divine, we all stand in judgment; none of us of ourselves is worthy of entering God's perfect light.

So here's the puzzle of our creation. God creates us as soulful beings so that we may join our Creator in perfect light. Yet we cannot of our own accord complete our transition from human to divine consciousness.

Just how does God help us solve this conundrum?

Transcendence. Unity. Transformation.

God invites us to transcend our present way of life, become one with the Spirit of God, and undergo a transformation that has paradox pulsating as its very heart.

Why are paradox and transformation so intimately linked?

Let's briefly digress.

Imagine Amelia Earhart taking off in an airplane from a western Pacific island, some remote atoll, and flying due east. Sooner or later she would find herself, paradoxically, journeying into the previous day. How can this apparent contradiction take place? Yesterday has already occurred; Ms. Earhart has already lived the fullness of its 24 hours.

The paradox that makes sense of the apparent contradiction is that our aviatrix has flown across the international date line, the globe's 180° meridian, which divides today from yesterday (if you're heading east, or today from tomorrow, if you're heading west).

Twelve Paradoxes

The Columbia Encyclopedia's fifth edition explains that we need the date line:

> ...to avoid a confusion that would otherwise result. For example, if an airplane were to travel westward with the sun, 24 hours would elapse as it circled the globe, but it would still be the same day for those in the airplane while it would be one day later for those on the ground below them. The same problem would arise if two travelers journeyed in opposite directions to a point on the opposite side of the earth, 180° of longitude distant. The eastward traveler would set his clock ahead 1 hour for each 15° of longitude, so that his clock would gain a total of 12 hours; the westward traveler would set his clock back 1 hour for each 15°, resulting in a total loss of 12 hours. The two clocks would therefore differ by 24 hours, or one calendar day. The apparent paradox is resolved by requiring that the traveler crossing the date line change his date, thus bringing the travelers into agreement when they meet.

Let's for a moment join Amelia Earhart in the cockpit just as she crosses the date line to look carefully at some of the fascinating properties that this meridian possesses. To begin, although the date line is only a concept, having no width or depth, it plays a vital role in helping us structure reality. It's particularly important to notice how the paradox of the date line reveals itself as Ms. Earhart undergoes her time transformation. As she cruises over this border, her white scarf flapping in the open cockpit window, Ms. Earhart also crosses a conceptual bridge that displays an eerie, apparently contradictory fusion of opposites.

For the international date line is in a sense:

- *Both* today *and* yesterday
- *Neither* today *nor* yesterday
- *Both* of the above
- *None* of the above.

The Paradox of Transformation

What really makes these bulleted items a brain teaser is their paradox: While some individual statements may contradict each other, at the same time, all in a sense are true; they represent the paradoxical unity of discrete, apparently contradictory entities. It is this very unity-in-diversity, though, that allows the date line to transform our famous pilot's flight into one of the previous day.

Crossing such a conceptual bridge also is necessary in order for us to make an important transformation — changing our path from one of destruction into one of enhancing life. Ascending this bridge, we transcend our tired, everyday perspective to undergo a kind of epiphany, or divinely inspired transformation, in which the Spirit of God changes our hearts forever. For a brief, eternal moment, we are enveloped in the light of God.

When this occurs, we find ourselves disoriented, for the markers that we use to define our world are not present; we are even beyond the realm of good and evil. There is only the light of God here, and although we may have some faint awareness that the shadow of evil exists somewhere outside, here as part of the light, we are far removed from it. For at this wonderful place, there is no good or evil, only the unity of God, the Alpha and Omega, the ecstasy of everlasting light.

We do not remain long at this transcendent place, however, for we still have an important role to play back in time and space. But our experience of becoming one with the light has changed us. When we return from the transcendent experience, we open our eyes and find that we have been transformed, that our feet now are walking down the other side of the bridge, where the path of embracing, enhancing, nurturing life begins.

We are Moses returning from the mountain. We are the Virgin Mary after speaking with the angel. We are Jesus after his transfiguration.

We have begun to awaken.

9

The Paradox of the Shadow

W hen we return from our transcendent, peak experience in the light of God's love, the afterglow dissipates sooner than we would like. It does not take long for us to be confronted again with the alienation and evil of our world and with our own sins. When this realization hits, we may wonder whether our transcendent experience was real or just a dream.

Those of the Eastern tradition assure us that it is our transcendent experience that is real and our worldly struggles illusion. Still, the experience of the passing century — the unimaginable cruelty of war, the genocide, the ethnic and religious hatred, the tyranny, the ecological devastation — make evil seem real enough. Our unshakable emotional pain and dread and fear seem clear enough evidence of our own individual alienation, as well.

Again we are presented with an apparent contradiction. For if evil is illusory, then how can it have such a pervasive effect? What can help us make sense of evil as illusion and God's light as reality?

Let's start by reflecting for a moment about the nature of light and darkness in our physical world. Light is active, true energy; darkness is but an absence, a lack of light. Hence the "presence" of darkness is an illusion.

Yet in our everyday lives, shadow can affect us just as if it were a presence. Seasonal affective disorder describes emotional depression caused by a lack of sunlight; being deprived of enough natural light can also weaken the immune system. If kept from sunlight for any appreciable time, most people fail to thrive and may even die. If most plant life on the earth was permanently deprived of sunlight, it would soon perish, along with the chain of animal life that depends on plants for food. Hence, the paradox of darkness is that we experience it as presence because of the profound effects that absence has on us.

We should briefly note that in the physical world, darkness is not always a bad thing. Shade protects us from the sun's searing rays. And who would deny the sublime reverie that a clear, starry night can inspire?

Spiritually speaking, darkness can also help us appreciate God's light. But we were not created to be children of darkness; thus we strive to emerge into God's light. Our hope for doing so?

Transcendence. Unity. Transformation.

Using God's gift of consciousness, we may transcend the darkness and join with the One True Light. Having emerged from the Light at the moment of our creation, we reunite with it at transcendent moments, those brief, eternal reflections of the Alpha and Omega union.

If we are faithful, death itself transforms from dread darkness into the most peaceful night as we ourselves become in unity with Alpha and Omega forever steadfast starlight.

10

The Paradox of Eden

Ne had the appil takè ben
Ne haddè never our lady
A ben heavenè quene.
Blessèd be the time
That appil takè was.
Therefore we moun singen,
Deo gracias!

Fifteenth century
English carol

To further explore the interplay between God, our true selves and our transitional shadow selves, we turn to the first book of the Bible, Genesis, and the story of Adam and Eve. For in this ancient allegory, our archetypal parents speak directly to us, their contemporary children. They teach us how our development as individuals — and evolution as a species — fit into the drama of light and darkness that is God's ongoing process of creation.

Before we begin, though, a note about how we will approach this famous story. As a child in Sunday school, I was taught that this story literally described humanity's — and nature's — fall from a golden age of perfection and immortality. Although some readers in this age of science may chuckle at this belief, even today many people still hold to this teaching, favored by the great church father, Augustine of Hippo.

This book, however, will take the approach championed by another church father, Saint Jerome, who said the story was an allegory. For if the revelations of science have taught us anything, it is that nothing in the dizzying dance of the cosmos ever was perfect, Adam and Eve and the Garden of Eden notwithstanding.

We won't be discussing Adam and Eve as literal, historical characters, nor will we attempt to surmise what lessons the Old Testament recorders of the story intended the ancient Hebrews to glean from the tale. Rather, we will view the Adam and Eve story as a tale of wisdom that speaks to each generation according to its own history, culture and understanding.

Hence, the following discussion complements this book's view of creation, evolution and our relationship with God, emphasizing Adam and Eve's many paradoxes.

Let's move on to a summary of the tale (refer to Genesis 2:15-24):

> God created Adam and Eve, the first human beings, from the dust of the earth in the Garden of Eden. Here the sinless couple lived in a state of primordial bliss, with God taking care of all their needs. But Satan entered the Garden in the form of a serpent and tempted Eve to eat from the tree of the knowledge of good and evil, from whose fruit God had forbidden her and Adam. Satan tantalized Eve with the promise that if she sampled this fruit, she would become "like God." Eve told Adam what the snake had said, and overwhelmed by curiosity, they tasted the tree's fruit.

> As soon as they did, though, Adam and Eve's eyes "were opened;" they realized that they were naked, and felt ashamed. So they sewed fig leaves together and wore them as aprons to cover themselves. When Adam and Eve heard God taking a

walk in the Garden, they tried to hide, but the Lord discovered them clothed and knew immediately that they had eaten from the forbidden tree. Realizing that Adam and Eve had become "like gods," knowing about good and evil, God feared that the errant pair would also gain immortality by eating from another supernatural tree in the Garden — the tree of life.

So God sewed Adam and Eve some skins for clothing and then banished them from the Garden, pronouncing that as a consequence of their actions, they and their children would know death. Moreover, Eve and all following generations of women would bear children in pain, and men would have to labor for food and shelter rather than having these needs provided by their Creator.

Finally, God posted an angel brandishing a flaming sword at the gate of the Garden so that humankind could never enter Eden again.

To start, Adam and Eve's eating from the tree of knowledge presents us with an important contradiction. On one hand, we think of moral knowledge as something that benefits mind and soul. (I hope that's why you're reading this book!) But on the other hand, for Adam and Eve, to gain such knowledge they must sin, disobey God.

As in our earlier analyses, let's start by examining the contradictory elements of the story. First, there's Adam and Eve's acquiring the knowledge of good and evil. According to our interpretation, this advance is positive.

For such knowledge shows that Adam and Eve have evolved into creatures of mind. Telling good from evil — moral awareness — reveals an advanced mode of abstract thinking.

How we act on such judgments plays a central role in our being human — in our personhood.

Keeping this in mind, we can begin to consider the negative side of the contradiction. For you have to be a creature of mind, a bona fide person, to achieve even the potential to sin. Had Adam and Eve been the most intelligent of trained dogs, or dolphins, or elephants, or even chimpanzees — primate cousins who share more than 98% of our DNA — we would not count their disobedience as sin. No, the moment Adam's bite liberates the forbidden fruit's delectable juices, the intention to be disobedient becomes the informed act of sin; the fruit of knowledge has offered Adam and Eve the awareness of wrongdoing.

Hence, by eating from the tree of knowledge, Adam and Eve are not just God's naughty pets. They are God's prodigal children. At the same time, paradoxically, this has its upside, for it means that they have moved up the evolutionary ladder out of the preconscious animal kingdom.

Why then does God forbid the fruit of knowledge to Adam and Eve? Is gaining the power of mind somehow tantamount to disobeying God? The answer paints a portrait of our spiritual dilemma.

To begin, as soon as they enter the realm of the mind, Adam and Eve realize that they are mortal. This is symbolized by our first parents fleeing the Garden, to be barred from the tree of life. Allegorically speaking, it has dawned on them that they're not going to be young and alive forever.

Next, Adam and Eve realize their mortality in a moral sense, as well. For with the ability to reason, they grasp not only the notion of goodness, but also such concepts as the ideal, perfection and the divine. When their minds snap together these various pieces, the completed puzzle reveals a terrifying scenario.

Namely, though "like the gods" both Adam and Eve have free will and moral judgment, unlike God, neither can live up even to their own standards, let alone those of divine perfection. Hence, to eat from the tree of knowledge is to recognize that one disobeys God, the Ideal.

In this, Adam and Eve reveal the legacy that Eden has left to us, their children. Our minds allow us to know good, at least to a degree, and even to do good. But because we are mortal, we succumb to sin and thus cannot be good no matter how hard we try.

In short, Adam and Eve teach us that consciousness, though a blessing, also puts us in a bind. As soon as we become aware of divine perfection's glory, our mortality pales before it. We turn our faces from its brilliance and flee God's presence.

Here we encounter another of Eden's apparent contradictions. For God banishes Adam and Eve from the Garden so that they cannot eat from the tree of eternal life. But this runs counter to what much of Western religion has come to believe is God's loving purpose for us — the reason that God creates us — to live forever with our Creator in heaven.

In other words, today we believe that God *wants us* to eat from the tree of eternal life. What is more, Christians believe that God sent us the Word, Jesus, to suffer and die *just so* we can eat from the tree of eternal life. Has Western religion changed so radically that its founders believed that God was determined to keep us away from eternal life while we today look at God as benevolently willing to suffer so that we might live forever?

Certainly, our view of God has changed over the millennia, as we've already discussed. But it's not changed in the sense that we once believed that God hated us, and now have come around to the realize that God loves us after all. One of the hallmarks of Western religion, in fact, is that we believe that despite our sins, which can exasperate, even anger our Creator, God remains on our side.

But if God still loves them, why do Adam and Eve go running in terror from God's presence in the Garden? I believe that this action reminds us that neither Adam and

Eve nor their children are able to embrace God's light and live forever of their own accord. Just because humanity has made the huge step out of the preconscious animal world doesn't mean that we have attained God consciousness. Although we are in the process of being created in God's image, we have only begun this journey of a thousand miles, and the dangers all along the way are formidable.

Just ask Adam and Eve. As they run weeping from the Garden, their story completes its movement from dilemma to paradox to irony. Our first parents realize that Satan was right about the tree of knowledge; by awakening into consciousness they have indeed entered the arena of the gods. What Satan had not told them, however, was that this step forward also would plunge them headlong into an abyss of alienation.

Our first parents' alienation reveals itself in several ways, beginning with their feeling ill at ease with their own bodies. Suddenly they feel the need to cover their nakedness. This betrays their discomfort with their sexuality, and forebodes the so-called "war between the sexes" that rages unabated today.

Next, Adam and Eve's expulsion from Eden's primordial splendor shows that they're alienated from God's ongoing handiwork, nature. As a newly conscious species, we do not continue in instinctual harmony with the natural world as do the sinless, preconscious creatures. The proof is in humanity's long history of being the bull in the china shop of nature's pristine harmony.

Our alienation betrays itself every time we use our advanced brains to disrupt the balance of natural life. So ingrained is our abusive attitude toward the earth that today many of us assume that economic well-being and ecological stewardship are necessarily at odds. Tragically, the contradiction of this destructive logic has no redeeming paradox —

the earth is the source of our happiness, our prosperity, our very survival; destroy the source, destroy ourselves — advanced technology has put such power in our hands.

Given this starkly negative aspect of the emerging human mind, one may begin to wonder if the paradox of Eden simply restates the hopeless paradox of this world. Do Adam and Eve simply lend weight to the view that human consciousness is at best an ironic accident, or at worst, divine error?

God has put the answer in our hands. Our Creator does not provide us with the blessing of mind only so that we might twist helplessly in the snare of our own sin. To the contrary, the gifts of consciousness and free will open for us the transcendent path, which unites us with God's creative, nurturing light, transforming us from shadow creatures of destruction. It is here that we discover God in ourselves; that in fact, we are partners with God — and with each other — in the process of our own creation, in forming a compassionate society that nurtures humanity and all life on earth.

As with the prodigal son, however, the paradox of Eden confirms that the first step toward awakening results in a stumble and fall. In our clumsy attempt to be like God, we offend God's holiness and disregard God as our Creator. We continue this discussion in the following chapter, for even as Eden harbors the potential for our self-destruction, it also opens the pathway to salvation.

The Paradox of the Soul

That I am human
I have in common with all people;
That I see and hear
And eat and drink
I share with all animals.
But that I am I is exclusively mine,
And belongs to me
And nobody else,
To no other person
Nor to an angel nor to God,
Except inasmuch as I am one with God.

Meister Eckhart

In the previous chapter, Adam and Eve introduced us to humanity's intellectual, instinctual and emotional transition from animal creature into mindful being. This is not a painless change; although the advent of reason allows us to make this evolutionary leap, we become dislocated from the animal kingdom's preconscious, instinctual harmony with the natural environment and its Creator. We lug like a millstone our alienation.

But what of our spirit, the human soul? What is the interplay between the emerging human mind and this aspect of our inner life? And just what is a soul, anyway?

To help us explore these intriguing questions, we turn

71

to a sage question posed to me when I was 15 years old by a schoolteacher of mine, Mr. Donald Reppa, who was challenging the religious fundamentalism that I was brandishing at the time. Mr. Reppa was exasperated by my belief that everyone would go to hell unless they accepted the Bible as a literal, set-in-stone account of history and accepted Jesus Christ as their personal savior. When I refused to budge on my view that God had consigned virtually everyone except those of my own denomination to eternal perdition, my teacher cried out in exasperation, "Don't you at least agree that there is something of God in every person?"

His question has lingered through more than three decades; to my shame, I believe that I answered "No." I thank God that much water has flowed under that particular bridge. In deference to my old teacher, I would like to share how I would answer him today. For these thoughts segue well into our discussion of the human soul.

Note that Mr. Reppa didn't ask whether I believed that there was something of God in *everything*, but in *every person*. While both these issues are notable — and related — there's an important difference between them. In defining this difference, I believe that we will gain some insight into that elusive concept that we call the human soul.

First let's examine the notion that there is something of God in everything. This restates the idea of God's immanence, the Holy Spirit's presence throughout all Creation. In the words of the Creeds, not only has everything "both seen and unseen" — all that exists in the physical and spiritual worlds — come from God; through the Holy Spirit, the Creator also remains present from the highest heaven to the depths of hell.

God's omnipresence, however, does not mean that created things are God or even that they are necessarily good — if a reputable history book or today's newspaper isn't available to confirm this, simply run a clean, damp cloth across the bathroom mirror and look deeply into the eyes that stare back at you.

On the most basic level, the Holy Spirit's presence within an entity means:

1. That it exists, and
2. That it is related to God and the rest of Creation through this common presence.

A third observation about the Spirit's presence is a most hopeful one. Even though God, by virtue of the gift of free will, allows created, mindful beings to do evil and thus bring judgment on themselves, the immanence of the Spirit holds forth the promise of each being's salvation. In other words, though our sense of human justice may make us feel certain that some people are absolutely, even eternally evil, our transcendent view reminds us that this is not so.

For, no matter how deeply hidden, some of God's ultimate good remains even in people who have done the cruelest things. Hence, they cannot be ultimately evil. Though our hearts may be made of stone, to paraphrase John the Baptist, with a single word, God can transform them into children of Abraham.

Therefore, no matter how deeply into the shadow of alienation any prodigal child may venture, God's immanent, loving presence offers forth the hope of rescue.

If you're like me, the prospect of universal redemption can seem unsatisfying; again, not insofar as it holds out hope for the salvation of oneself. It's other people getting off the hook that I fret about. I have a vengeful side that *relishes* the thought of the cruel, unrepentant, purveyors of suffering, destruction and death rotting in hell forever, the Hitlers and Stalins and Pol Pots. (Truth be told, one or two former supervisors also come to mind!)

But if you will join me for a moment to set aside anger and re-enter the cooler, transcendent plain, we encounter some fascinating insights. For, from this perspective, we happen upon the soul. And we find that it represents an advanced state of existence in God's continuum of creation.

Although not in these words, the concept of God's creative continuum has been percolating throughout previous pages. For instance, our discussion of the mind's evolution in the Adam and Eve story gave us a glimpse at humanity's special place among the animals in the Great Circle of Creation. To set the stage for our discussion of the soul, however, we need to go back to the beginning.

Not the beginning of life on earth or of the earth itself or even of its solar system. We must return to the dawn of the cosmos. So let's summarize, step by step, what we've already surmised about cosmic creation as it has developed since even before the fateful microsecond that ushered in the Big Bang:

1. The unity of God. The state of spiritual grace that precedes Creation.
2. Chaos. Into nothingness, the first milliseconds of cosmic creation and the Big Bang occur.
3. Space, time, energy and matter. The order that almost immediately begins to take shape out of the Big Bang's chaos. Order is reflected by the "laws of nature," such as gravitational properties, the speed of light, the laws of thermodynamics, atomic properties — and others, some perhaps yet to be discovered — that shape the cosmos.
4. Bios. On earth, at least, nature's laws allow for the Spirit in matter to awaken into next level of creation, sentient, preconscious, biological life. Each individual member of life expresses its own spirit.

5. Preconscious awareness. Higher animal life forms such as insects, reptiles, amphibians, birds and mammals develop limited thinking ability to complement their instincts and reflexes. They become individuals with their own "personalities."

6. Self-consciousness/alienation. The advent of the senses and abstract thinking allows for self-awareness and reason. While a major evolutionary advance, self-consciousness in human life coincides with spiritual alienation, which can be so destructive as to threaten the species.

The final two steps, implied in earlier chapters, will now be discussed in more detail. They include:

7. Redemption. God further hones the gift of consciousness, using it to invite mindful beings out of the shadow of alienation and back into divine light. Those who accept this invitation transcend their own fears and egocentric needs and serve God, nurturing each other and all life. Given the destructive potential of technology, the survival of the species may depend on embracing God's redemption.

8. Reunion with God. The gift of consciousness allows redeemed life to realize unity with God — and in God's immanent unity, with all Creation. This oneness transcends even biological death. In fact, biological death culminates God's creative process, as life returns to its Source in the unity of Alpha and Omega.

Just where, though, does the human soul fit into this scenario? The answer resides at the fourth level of existence: bios. On earth, within this level alone we find myriad gradations of existence among more than 30 million species.

Within the animal kingdom itself we find a vast spectrum of intelligence and awareness, from common slugs to species *Homo sapiens.*

Yet no matter how profound the differences may be between the varied forms of bios, there appears to be a special difference between living and nonliving entities. I believe that it is God's presence made manifest in a very special way — as the Spirit within matter is gifted with the holy mystery of its own individual spirit. So yes, Mr. Reppa, I do believe that God is present in everything, and in a special way with living things.

"But you haven't fully answered my question," I can almost hear my teacher pressing on, accompanied by that intense look he always would get in his eye when he sensed that he was nudging his student over the cusp of a new insight. "So, what distinguishes the human soul from the spirits of other creatures?"

In the Western tradition, we pay lip service to the "sanctity of all life," but in practice, give little consideration to the spirits of living things other than people. In fact, we tend to view other species as little more than commodities for our food, clothing, medicine, entertainment or economic exploitation. The implication is that if the species in question does not provide a direct benefit to humanity, it is expendable — even to extinction.

Eastern and native religions, however, tend to reverence God's presence in all life. They emphasize not that other species are different from our own, but that we humans are kindred with other forms of life. We even have the foundations for such a view in the Western tradition, for the unity-in-diversity of life may reflect the unity-in-diversity of our Creator.

If it is the direct presence of the Holy Spirit that awakens life within matter, then God does not so much create and destroy life throughout Creation, but shares life as an eternal, uniquely divine gift. When bios ends, the gift returns to the Giver. It is this shared holiness that makes all life sacred.

With this we come very close in our quest for the human soul. We set the final stage with two statements:

1. Each living thing has its own individual spirit, a spirit that is paradoxically shared with God.
2. Since this spiritual aspect of life makes it eternal, then in an important sense, life is of itself transcendent, and not only of the physical, temporal, and hence "illusory" world.

Prepare, then, for the debut of the soul, which occurs when preconscious awareness becomes consciousness. With the advent of the mind and full realization that "I am," a living spirit becomes forever wedded to consciousness. Hence, a soul is a spirit that has been eternally awakened.

Thus, we discover another level of meaning to the Adam and Eve tale: With consciousness, not only is a mind born, but an immortal soul. The preconscious animal spirit becomes an eternal person "like the gods," or more accurately, like the God who declared to Moses, "I am the I am." As implied by the Meister Eckhart epigraph that leads this chapter, from the moment Adam and Eve whisper to themselves, "I am," they show us what it means to be created in God's image.

So finally, Mr. Reppa, here is my answer. "Yes, there is something profoundly of God in every human being: first existence, then life, consciousness and finally soul."

Yet there remains a missing piece to the puzzle. For this chapter is not entitled, "The Advent of the Soul," but "The Paradox of the Soul." What, then, is the apparent contradiction that evokes this paradox?

Both the contradiction and the paradox reside with our archetypal parents, Adam and Eve, and so to conclude this chapter, we again return to their story.

We had originally considered how Adam and Eve teach us that on a psychological level, consciousness brings with it an awareness of our mortality. We realize that we are creatures with a beginning, a middle and an end. Yet we have just discussed how on a spiritual level, consciousness makes us eternally aware and therefore immortal. How can we possibly have it both ways? How can we be both mortal creatures and immortal beings?

There's the rub. As we venture with Adam and Eve across the threshold of consciousness, we realize that we indeed are both mortal and immortal. We are immortal souls, with attendant immortal longings, who animate mortal bodies whose needs and joys, striving and contentment, health and illness are one with our spiritual lives.

Such is the sometimes wonderful, sometimes agonizing paradox of the human soul. Our pursuit of its mystery will continue in the following chapter.

12

The Paradox of Humanity

In this chapter our archetypal parents, Adam and Eve, continue to instruct us about the human soul, which they debuted in the Garden of Eden. The soul helps us to accept an idea which from a mechanistic, Newtonian view seems virtually impossible, that people as physical entities can have free will.

Varied academic and political camps have spent much of the passing century either striving to prove that free will was not possible, or assuming that it was, trying to stamp it out. Certainly advocates of fascism, communism and other totalitarian systems taught that human beings could be hammered into molds designed by social architects. Sigmund Freud's deterministic view of human behavior also has had a significant influence on twentieth-century thought.

Perhaps the high water mark for the scientific belief in mechanistic human behavior came in the mid-twentieth century, when a school of behavioral psychologists headed by the late B.F. Skinner viewed human behavior as absolutely determined by physical wiring and environment. The title of one of Skinner's best sellers, *Beyond Freedom and Dignity*, indicates his belief that such lofty ideas were actually impediments to human progress because personal autonomy is an illusion.

As the millennium approached, scientific discoveries from the cosmic to the quantum levels put to rest the purely mechanistic theories of how the universe — and human beings — work. Keith Ward discusses this in "Religion and the Scientific World-View," a chapter in *A Vision to Pursue: Beyond the Crisis in Christianity.* As for how science has come to view the laws of nature, he writes:

> . . . the basic laws of physics, like the conservation laws, are laws which set limits to what can happen, rather than determining laws, which compel just one thing to happen. If the fundamental laws of nature state basic parameters of physical change, then there remains a sort of indeterminateness in the structure of the universe which introduces the possibility of genuine novelty and unpredictability in detail. Furthermore, the law-like behavior of physical bodies seems to have a quality of openness to wider fields of influence or to emergent principles of behavior. Indeed, the laws themselves are emergent; they emerge from more primeval states of the universe just after the Big Bang which started the whole process going.

This view complements the theology of an immanent God who is reflected in divine Creation, the universe. Because the Spirit of God is free and therefore unpredictable, the Spirit's omnipresence implies an inherent freedom in Creation. And because the Spirit represents the ultimate life, its pervasive presence implies an ever-changing — organic — universe.

Hence, the immanence of the Spirit betrays such designations as organic and inorganic as artificial. All the cosmos, from its birth until its death, moves, changes, grows, evolves, emerges, and in this sense is organic; alive. Under the right conditions, what we commonly think of as life appears out of "lifeless" matter and energy, entities that science had long assumed were inorganic. Now we begin to understand this apparent contradiction instead as a reflection of the divine paradox; in the immanent presence of the Spirit, life awakens from a nascent form on an organic continuum that begins at the creation of the universe.

We had previously alluded to John the Baptist's prophetic pronouncement that God could transform stones into children of Abraham. Because these Palestinian stones are graced with the Spirit within them, God need not perform a miracle to accomplish this. For the stones are already children of Abraham waiting to be awakened.

The New Testament records two instances of Jesus raising people from the dead; one involving a young girl, another his friend Lazarus. In both stories, Jesus refers to the dead people as sleeping; each time his comment is met with the derisive laughter of irony. And in both stories those who witness the miracles of awakening see ironic contradiction revealed as liberating paradox.

If the very stars and planets of the cosmos and the stones of Palestine have their freedom, no less do we as conscious, soulful beings. Not only do we live in an unpredictable world, but also, as we grow in the Spirit, we become aware that our soul reflects our Creator in an important way. As an indestructible, eternally living entity, the soul is present both in the temporal, worldly plain, and in another, transcendent dimension, that "of the gods." Hence, part of us never leaves the timeless transcendent, where the rules of physical cause and effect do not have the ultimate influence over our personality or our actions.

We are physical creatures and soulful beings mysteriously united in diversity by the Spirit that suffuses all that we are. So we are not just mechanical toys whose wiring compels us to react to our environment in programmed or reflexive ways. Neither are we robots of flesh that are animated by an otherwise aloof and autonomous mind. Rather, we are organic beings who, in awakening, are constantly shaping our own thoughts, behavior, environment and future.

Keith Ward eloquently states how such a view complements an emergent theology:

> Humans can be seen, not as alienated parts of a grand machine, but as points of emerging responsibility, creativity, understanding and self-control within the emergent world-process. God will not be the supreme, but strangely indifferent clock-maker of eighteenth-century theology or the autocratic monarch of some biblical religion. God will be seen as one who creates primal energy and then draws from it communities of persons who are capable of growth towards full consciousness, understanding, happiness and responsible creativity. God will be an empowering ideal, not a tyrant or a watch-maker; and the revelations of divine nature and purpose which occur in religious experience will be the present glimpses of our future goal and of a cosmic ideal which can empower our own efforts to achieve it.

Professor Ward writes of empowerment tempered by responsibility and self-control. In this he joins Rabbi Harold Kushner, C. S. Lewis and Archibald MacLeish in emphasizing how central free choice is to our spiritual growth. We cannot grow without moral integrity, and freedom allows us to develop this virtue. Hence, we require a moral sense to be truly human.

Our sinfulness creates a dilemma for us, though; since none of us is truly moral, then neither are we fully human, at least in the most noble sense. Our destructive behavior shows that we are not fully mature in our humanity. This immaturity goes hand-in-hand with the alienation that is Adam and Eve's legacy.

So what further insights do our archetypal parents offer us their children, created to be free yet living like slaves to sin? Let's revisit their story for a final time to find out.

As their saga unfolds, our first parents' behavior progresses from a happy, childlike, naive state into one of rebellion against their Parent, who loves them dearly. What is more, they feel ill at ease with their own bodies and sexuality. Finally, their guilt over such feelings transforms even paradise into a place of fear, persecution and rejection; they begin to misperceive their Parent as an angry, tyrannical judge.

Many parents with teen-agers will nod their heads knowingly. For I have just described the classic emotions of adolescence. It's no coincidence, for Adam and Eve teach us of a kind of spiritual adolescence that is humanity's paradox.

Adolescent girls and boys, though journeying toward maturity, have not quite reached their destination. They are caught amidst a painful transition. Though no longer children, they are not yet adults; though expected to act responsibly, they are not allowed full adult privileges.

The Adam and Eve allegory, the story of our awakening into consciousness, reveals that in the fashion of adolescence, all humanity is in a paradoxical state of transition. We are no longer preconscious animals, yet are still physical; though eternally conscious souls, we are not entirely spiritual, either.

Our venture into consciousness and its accompanying spiritual transition means that we find ourselves dislocated, existing paradoxically both "here" as temporal, physical beings and "there" as eternal souls, and yet not wholly in either state. We as soulful creatures are in the midst of being created by God, and though we each have divine longings, spiritual darkness remains a part of us — body, mind and soul — and must be transformed into the loving light of the divine for us to be fulfilled.

In other words, until we are fully created, that is, returned to God as mature spiritual beings, we remain very much amidst the struggle in which God is creating order out of the chaos that emerged at the Big Bang, and is both around us, physically, in our universe, and within us, morally and spiritually.

How we react to this struggle defines our character. We may become engulfed by our own internal chaos and add to the emotional and spiritual chaos of others. We can contribute to physical chaos directly by harming others in body or disrupting the balance of the earth, or we can do it indirectly, by becoming so self-absorbed that we turn a blind eye to others or to the destruction of our planet.

Such reactions may help explain why, though we are created as reflections of a loving God, we find ourselves willing to consign our neighbor to the chaos of poverty, ignorance, homelessness and starvation. And why, even as our sexuality can reflect the deepest and most tender aspects of our love, we so often express it unloving ways.

Our alienation from nature cries out when we ravage the earth, our home, and destroy the living environment put into our care by God. Perhaps our inner chaos manifests itself most blatantly when we show no respect for kindred life, destroying natural habitats, wiping out entire species.

Suburban sprawl. Clear cutting forests. Slash and burn farming. Over-fishing. Uncontrolled use of fossil fuels. It's all reminiscent of the not-so-golden rule of communal property that I discovered when I lived in various group settings before I married: "What's mine is mine and what's everybody's is nobody's." Translated into the point at hand: "You want to save nature? Then you make the sacrifice."

Since we as conscious beings are responsible for our actions, one spiritual aspect of the Adam and Eve story takes on sobering overtones. For as eternal beings, our flight from God's love has ramifications even after we leave bios behind. Our moral accountability, the stuff of that transcendent, eternal plain, does not stop with biological life, the memories of our children, or even the judgment of history; it continues through when we stand in judgment before our Maker.

There are those who find the concept of hell embarrassing, archaic, intolerant, or illogical in the face of a loving Creator, and thus have abandoned it. I feel that this is mistaken. For who has not witnessed hell here on earth, many of us firsthand?

Ask any survivor of the many concentration camps, gulags or killing fields for which our century will forever be notorious. Ask any soldier who has come under aerial attack or civilian who has been maimed by the terrorist's bomb. Ask those whose families have suffered genocide in Africa or ethnic cleansing in the Balkans. Ask American Indians living impoverished on reservations or people living under the bondage of slavery in North Africa. Ask the prisoner on death row who has been falsely or mistakenly convicted.

Hell, a state of mind, is hence a spiritual state. Those who cause such inexpressible suffering on the earth betray that they have chosen to run away, rather than embrace the open arms of God. Do such souls abruptly shed their alienation and suddenly reverse course when they leave this world for the next? I believe that their darkness remains.

What then of our chronic alienation, the universal human imperfection described in the Adam and Eve story? Does this seal the destiny of all of us in the hell of an angry God? Thankfully, the answer is no.

However lost we may become, God has not made us for darkness, but for the light. And paradoxically, the very punishments handed down by God at the end of the Adam and Eve allegory help us to understand this.

Our first glimmer of hope reveals itself in how God does not decide to punish Adam and Eve. Our Creator does not destroy humanity in its infancy, which would be the merciful thing to do if we were all doomed to eternal misery. Instead, God displays the most tender love by sewing Adam and Eve clothes so that they may survive the harsher climes outside Eden.

In this symbolic action God prepares us for the challenges beyond Eden's preconscious world. And here's where the story's punishments come in. Described as hard work for men and painful childbirth for women, on thoughtful inspection, these images may not shame us but paradoxically serve as signposts to guide us home.

Punishments that instill hope? Rejection from a wonderful garden that puts us on the road to fulfillment? To fathom this paradox, we must return to our watchwords.

Transcendence. Unity. Transformation.

If we transcend the fatigue of hard work and the excruciating pain that can accompany the birth of a child, we are left with the wholeness and sense of satisfaction that our efforts can bring. Why do we work hard? To care for our families, advance our careers, or make the world a better place; even the very wealthy work to give their lives meaning. And why — even when living in a culture that affords them a choice — do so most women bear children? So that they can bring forth the greatest of all blessings, new life.

Just as hard work or childbirth involves us totally, so does God invite us to be totally involved in our own creation. We can choose freely whether to walk toward the light or the darkness, in positive or negative faith, a commitment that involves decisions that we make every day. We grow in the Spirit — as individuals, as a society, as the human race — if we choose the path of light that our Creator has laid before us.

The Adam and Eve tale does make it clear that this path involves struggle. Our daily errors in judgment, our

The Paradox of Humanity

sins large and small may cause us to stumble often, almost constantly. But if we are grounded in a faithful, prayerful relationship with God, we do not despair. We get up and dust ourselves off time after time to continue our trek toward the light.

As we continue along this path, we find ourselves gradually transcending self-centeredness and anger and envy and vengefulness and fear. We become ever more one with the Source of life and sharing and love. And in this union we are transformed.

But we cannot accomplish this on our own. We must work with God. To pose the question using the imagery of the Adam and Eve story, how best do we invite the Holy Spirit to be our taskmaster and midwife?

In Part Two, The Great Awakening, we pursue the answers to these questions.

The Great Awakening

The Third
Great Awakening

In the beginning was the Word,
and the Word was with God,
and the Word was God.
He was in the beginning with God.
All things came into being through him,
and without him not one thing came into being.
What has come into being in him was life,
and the life was the light of all people.
The light shines in the darkness,
and the darkness did not overcome it.

John 1:1-5

B y now, having read through the Twelve Paradoxes, the reader should not be surprised that this book has been entitled, *In Pursuit of the Divine Paradox*. But what about *Awakening*, the first part of the title? Fear not, dear reader, for Part II of the book is entitled, "The Great Awakening."

This should not be confused with the First Great Awakening, an evangelical Christian movement born by a sermon delivered by Jonathan Edwards in 1734 in Northampton, Massachusetts, and which helped inspire the founding of many of this country's great colleges and universities. Nor does it refer to the Second Great Awakening, a revival movement with similar import on the spiritual life of the United States in the late 1820s and early 1830s. Beginning in upstate New York, this religious movement increased church membership by 100,000 in a single year and is credited by historians with having spawned social movements ranging from temperance and abolition to anti-dueling, moral reform, public education and public philanthropy.

Rather, Part II refers to the Third Great Awakening, the revolution in spiritual awareness that we in the United States are undergoing even as I write these words. Worship attendance is up, whether in the mainline or evangelical denominations, or in the synagogues. The Pentecostal movement continues growing, both within denominational and independent churches.

The women's rights and women's liberation movement has segued into the women's spirituality movement. Spiritual aspects of healing are returning to the medical arts and to psychology. There are strong spiritual overtones in growing ecological awareness, and where people have found traditional venues wanting, house churches and prayer groups have taken root.

Part II: The Great Awakening invites Christians and all people of faith to focus this energy, to intentionally deepen our relationship with God, for our own good and so that life on the planet may flourish. Part II beckons readers to the Third Age of spirituality, in which people of all faiths come to respect the validity and spiritual power of each other's beliefs and work together for peace and freedom and loving stewardship of the earth. Finally, Part II urges readers to approach the dawn of the new millennium as an unprecedented chance to establish loving, compassionate human relationships worldwide.

The Third Great Awakening

With the cusp of the millennium upon us, much speculation has developed regarding Christian apocalyptic beliefs about the return of Christ, based on scriptural passages such as Revelations Chapter 20. Such thought can be divided up into:

- premillennial, favored by many Christian evangelicals and Pentecostals, which posits that Christ will come in person to rule a new heaven and a new earth in peace for one thousand years.

- postmillennial, in vogue with many Christians from the time of St. Augustine in the fifth century until the nineteenth century, and part of the inspiration for the first two Great Awakenings. This belief suggests that the teachings of Christ will hold such sway of themselves that they will usher in the thousand years of peace.

- amillennial, including most contemporary Roman Catholic and mainline Protestant scholars, who say that John's reference in Revelation to the binding of Satan for a thousand years has some more subtle, symbolic meaning than either the pre- or postmillennialists would allow.

While Part II: The Great Awakening is mostly postmillennial in approach, it does contain elements of all three beliefs. It is amillennial in that it proposes a symbolic approach to the binding up of Satan and the thousand years of peace. Yet Part II is premillennial to the extent that it discusses the coming of Christ today as a very real spiritual presence. Finally, Part II is postmillennial in that it does not portend the imminent end of the world, but rather, tells of our opportunity to commence with the Third Great Awakening, an enlightened era of peace and compassion —

and what better evidence could we hope for that Satan has been bound in chains?

There have been glimmerings of the awakening theme even throughout Part I of this book; for example, in tracing God's cosmic creative process to the evolution of the human mind. With the dawn of consciousness, we discover our small, flickering part in the universe's awakening into self-awareness.

Part II will deal less with Creation awakening to itself, though, and more with us, humanity, awakening to Creation. At the border of the third millennium, we find ourselves holding a much different view of the cosmos than was held by the writers of the Bible, or even by the Church Fathers. Today we face a universe that is far older, vaster and more complex than anything Western scholars had imagined even a century ago.

How far we have come from Aristotle's earth-centered universe with the discovery that our planet is little more than a single bauble dangling on the necklace of the sun, itself a minor star. And our humble star is but one of many billions dancing within but one of 200 billion galaxies, all rushing outward in a rapidly expanding universe.

Year after year today's scientists with the assistance of volunteers on the Internet, comb the sky, searching for some electronic signal of intelligent life on another planet, perhaps even more advanced than our own. This prospect raises profound questions for all religious traditions, such as: How well do our teachings accommodate the possibility of life on other planets? Of intelligent life? Of life far more sophisticated than our own? And for Christians: How could our theology of the Cosmic Christ, of a human Jesus as an eternal king with a hand in the very making of the universe, still be considered seriously?

CHAPTER 13

The Third Great Awakening

The answer may be a journey of myriad light years. But it still begins with the single, humble step that Adam and Eve ventured out of Eden and into the realm of human consciousness. So please turn the page.

The adventure continues.

The New Adam

As we concluded Part I, Adam and Eve had bequeathed to us quite a dilemma. They challenged us, their children, to achieve our final stage of spiritual evolution, reunion with God; yet they also saddled us with a legacy of alienation that compels us to flee this fulfillment.

Is it possible for us to cut this Gordian knot? I believe it is, but only with some help from our familiar watchwords: Transcendence. Unity. Transformation.

Part II suggests that God sends us a new Adam — Jesus of Nazareth — to help us transcend our mortal dilemma and thus complete what Adam and Eve were only able to begin. For as part of the ongoing process of Creation, God intervenes directly to reconcile us with the divine unity by having a woman conceive a child not by another human being, but by the power of the Holy Spirit. By this extraordinary act, the unity between us and our Creator is expressed even more intimately than if we were partners in marriage. God's spiritual marriage with humanity opens the door for us prodigal children to begin all over again in our dealings both with our Maker and Creation.

Before we pursue this discussion, though, we must examine some of the apparent contradictions that this view of the Christ presents. Perhaps most obvious is the virgin birth itself, which runs counter to all of our everyday experience about conceiving a child. There's also the traditional Jewish understanding of the Messiah as a political ruler, a military hero who, like David, should establish Israel as a superpower. Only this Son of David would establish forever a government ruled by God's righteousness.

Another two important contradictions:

> *The contradiction of human versus divine nature.* Given his unique parentage, is Jesus a human being or divine?

> *The contradiction of overcoming biological death.* After Jesus' death, he appears to his disciples after two days in the tomb. Then after 40 days he physically ascends into heaven. This certainly flies in the face of everyday experience.

We could agree with some theologians who say, well after all, most of what was recorded about Jesus was written many years after his life on earth. Thus it was easy for the supernatural aspects of his story to snowball as evangelists tried ever harder over the years to convince new audiences just how special Jesus was. These scholars argue that we don't really need to accept a supernatural answer to such apparent contradictions — either to nature or everyday experience — in order to believe that Jesus should be venerated as the Child of God.

It's a very compelling and faithful point of view. But what if we didn't have to deal with the supernatural aspects of Jesus' personality as an embarrassment? What if overarching these apparent contradictions were a paradox — the divine paradox — to which our watchwords would apply in their most profound way? To my mind this may offer us a scenario that preserves the orthodox, supernatural aspects of

The New Adam

Jesus' story in a way that is consistent with a contemporary understanding of how God works in the universe.

For example, according to our watchwords, in conceiving Jesus, Mary was called by God to transcend her earthly nature and achieve spiritual union with her Creator. In this union, she was transformed in miraculous pregnancy.

We can also understand the relationship of the Holy Spirit and Mary as the Transcendent, paradoxically, coming down to us and in this union transforming not only Mary, but all humanity.

Such ideas actually may be easier for me to accept than another that I have come to embrace — that 12 billion years ago, you and I and the farthest quasar of the universe were nestled cozily together in a womb that was smaller than the nucleus of an atom! I would also find it less startling that for us, Adam and Eve's children, the union between Mary and the Holy Spirit results in the very transformation that humanity requires to achieve its final stage of spiritual evolution, reunion with God. We will return to all this later in Part II.

Discussing such issues will hinge on the paradoxical notion of the Transcendent becoming present to us. For it was not only Jesus' conception, but his entire life and death with us that reveal his transcendent nature. And it is this paradox of transcendent presence that generates its own kind of logic underlying some of the odd, apparent contradictions that surround Jesus as the Christ.

For instance, the divinely conceived Jesus, neither God nor human, is paradoxically both God and human. Moreover, this co-equal person of the all-powerful God comes to us as a helpless child to teach us the very nature of divine love.

This child embodies God's limiting of divine power to allow us the freedom to love. Hence, as a transcendent human being, Jesus serves as a divine example of loving discipline and sacrifice.

Time and again throughout the New Testament we are symbolically reminded that Jesus is Transcendence having come down to us. To wit, at the transfiguration, itself a transcendent experience, the Creator calls Jesus "my son, my Chosen."

Transcendence. Unity. Transformation.

In the transfiguration, the unity of Jesus and the Creator is made manifest. Jesus undergoes a transformation in which he is taken up into a cloud and returns with his face glowing as brightly as snow in the sun, an obvious reference to Moses as he came down from Mount Sinai with the Ten Commandments — the result of yet another transcendent experience.

An additional sign of transcendence is Jesus' resurrection — the transcendence of bios. After two days in the tomb, Christ's unity with God again is revealed as he, Jesus, returns in a transformed body that becomes reunified with the Creator in his ascent into heaven.

Transcendence. Unity. Transformation.

In Jesus' ascension, he transcends biological life. He transcends the earth and the cosmos. In this he enters and thus is reunited with the direct presence of the Creator through the Holy Spirit.

But by so returning to the Creator, another unity is fulfilled as well, the unity of the whole in its completion. In ascending into heaven, Christ completes the universal evolutionary cycle of the human spirit.

Let's examine this striking statement in more detail. C. S. Lewis points out that by being the first human being to complete this spiritual course, Jesus traces the entire path of human evolution within the span of a single lifetime. After the moment he is begotten of the Holy Spirit, Jesus, as does all human embryonic life, traces prehuman evolution from one of the simplest forms of life, a single cell, through our development from a fishlike creature with gills and a tail in the saline liquid environment of the womb, through full human development and birth as a baby. After he is born, Jesus matures into adulthood and passes through the transitions of death and resurrection; finally, he returns to heaven as the first spiritually mature human being. Therein lies the entire evolutionary cycle of humanity, from the alpha of a single cell that has life breathed into it by the Holy Spirit, through the omega of spiritual maturity, transcending humanity itself in reunion with the Creator.

Therefore, by being the first to complete the full cycle of human development, Jesus is able to serve as a kind of bridge that reunites an alienated, incomplete, adolescent humanity with its Creator. He acts as the final arc who through his own transformation closes the Great Circle of Creation for our species. In the unity of God, the transcendent Christ is revealed as both the totality and fulfillment of human creation/evolution.

By himself embodying this holy, transcendent bridge, Jesus again reflects the divine unity and its paradox: Alpha and Omega, Christ unites the God who has been within us from our beginning with the God outside us who waits at our journey's end. In Christ, our existence meets its fulfillment at the point of its beginning — just as God, the Alpha and the Omega of all Creation, reveals the divine unity at the End of Days.

In his letter to the Ephesians, the Apostle Paul makes it clear that Christ completes the cycle of human existence not for himself alone, but so that we may follow to our own fulfillment:

> until all of us come to the unity of the faith and of the knowledge of the Son of God, to maturity, to the measure of the full stature of Christ . . .
>
> *Ephesians 4:13*

and thereby transcend and be transformed:

> . . . to know the love of Christ that surpasses knowledge, so that you may be filled with all the fullness of God.
>
> *Ephesians 3:19*

Hence, just as the mythical Adam and Eve begin the saga of human consciousness in alienation, Jesus of Nazareth becomes a second and last Adam who fulfills it in glory:

> Thus it is written, "The first man, Adam, became a living being"; the last Adam became a life-giving spirit. But it is not the spiritual that is first, but the physical and then the spiritual . . . Just we have borne the image of the man of dust, we will also bear the image of the man of heaven.
>
> *I Corinthians 15:45-46,48*

Both Adams introduce humanity to the next level of spiritual evolution. Adam and Eve bring us from the pre-conscious spiritual "childhood" of the animals to the level of consciousness and soul, a kind of spiritual adolescence that also involves our temporary alienation from God. Christ, the last Adam, blazes a trail for us from this adolescence to spiritual maturity and permanent reconciliation with God.

In Paul's first letter to the Corinthians we see another scriptural parallel between the first Adam and the last. For in referring to Christ as the last Adam, Paul uses both clothing and work imagery as the Adam and Eve tale does, only with twist. Notice how with his clothing imagery, Paul writes not of humanity's shame as with the Genesis story, but of humanity's fulfillment.

> When this perishable body puts on imperishability, and this mortal body puts on immortality, then the saying that is written will be fulfilled:
> "Death has been swallowed up in victory."
> "Where, O death, is your victory?
> Where, O death, is your sting?"
>
> *I Corinthians 15:54-55*

Paul's account also shares work imagery with the Adam and Eve tale. Only by contrast to the story of the first Adam, this imagery has been transformed from allegorical punishment into literal blessing:

> Therefore, my beloved, be steadfast, immovable; always excelling in the work of the Lord, because you know that in the Lord your labor is not in vain.
>
> *I Corinthians 15:58*

In summary, while our first parents take us a step up the evolutionary ladder into consciousness, this paradoxically brings about alienation and human evil. When Jesus willingly and lovingly sacrifices his life to such evil, Christ transcends by his death and resurrection to redeem and enlighten all people — to introduce us to our next evolutionary level — and so fulfill human destiny. Thus, by the call of God's grace, *in pursuing the divine paradox we cross the bridge of positive transformation and transcend the paradox of this world.*

Transcendence. Unity. Transformation.

In Jesus Christ are we thus fulfilled.

CHAPTER 15

The New Eden

Jesus, our fulfillment and completeness; Christ, the essential element of divine Creation that allows every person to achieve the unity of wholeness. This theme reverberates far beyond our personal relationship with God. For alienation does not just stunt our spiritual growth as individuals; it also threatens humanity and much of the very life on this planet.

The advent of space travel has allowed us a transcendent view of the earth. From this perspective far above the atmosphere, we perceive the balance of life on earth as a kind of Eden. We begin to realize that the Creator has not driven us out of the Garden at all; in our alienation, we are destroying Eden, which God in divine love has left us free to do.

Hence, it is morally incumbent on Adam and Eve's children to make the most of the fruits of wisdom that the Garden has offered us. We must act now to save our home. Pleading ignorance is no longer an option.

Keeping this in mind, we ask ourselves if there is a liberating paradox that can save us from own destructive contradictions.

Just what is humanity's central contradiction, anyway, at least from a faithful person's point of view? I suggest it is that we're supposedly being created in God's image, no matter how ungodly our behavior may seem at times. If our minds cannot somehow come to terms with the paradox of our being created to be holy and yet sometimes acting like Satan, the faithful face the danger of tearing themselves psychically apart.

This can happen in one of two ways.

In the first, we fixate on the former half of the contradiction — us as God's image — and view ourselves as little gods. In other words, "We (whatever group we identify with) are created in God's image; therefore, though we may have our faults, it's others who are the *real* sinners." Denying our own fundamental flaw, we think of ourselves as the saints who are morally above those who do not believe as we do, and endeavor to convert or destroy anyone outside our group. In satanic self-righteousness, we create barriers in our hearts against the outsiders, justifying our every action against them, no matter how cruel, as serving a "higher good," or even God.

In the second kind of hurtful attitude, we wallow in the latter half of the contradiction — that we can't be righteous no matter how hard we try. If we follow this path, we may in despair lead nihilistic lives, seeking to keep ourselves drunk on the wine of pleasure, power and wealth. "Since we're all corrupt and doomed, why not at least have fun sinning?"

We may also succumb to our own sinfulness by directing this negative energy inward, fostering debilitating guilt and self-hatred. We may focus this only on ourselves, or perhaps cast a wide beam across all humanity. "How could God possibly love such a loathsome creature such as myself?" we ask. Or perhaps, "If there really were a loving God, why would our Creator make a race with such a passion for exploitation, cruelty and death?"

How can believers realize and assimilate the paradox of our situation? We must put the Satan that is within ourselves behind us. But how?

Perhaps if we realize that we are not yet fully created. Perhaps if we can come to accept that our spiritual evolution means that we are *in the process of being created* in God's image through our biological lives. If this were so, we should actually expect ourselves to fall as immature, incomplete spiritual beings, much as a baby must repeatedly fall as it learns to walk.

Jesus teaches that no matter how many times we fall in a moral sense — no matter how far we are from being completely created in God — if we truly repent, our Creator will forgive us. Not because the author of the universe is a soft-hearted old fool or a glutton for punishment, but because our Maker wants to finish creating every one of us. What is more, since every person is a work in progress, part of our faithful struggle is to allow ourselves mercy and to forgive others when they sin against us, too.

Just how long does the creation of human soul take? Heaven only knows what the process may have involved for any of us individually before we were born. As for this life-time, Jesus assures us that once we commit our hearts to God, our struggle toward spiritual fulfillment will culminate just as bios ends for each of us.

Transcendence. Unity. Transformation.

Jesus invites us to transcend our fears and our despair, to enter into a spiritual union with him and be transformed. In this transformation, the Holy Spirit completes our creation, allowing us to lead lives of integrity, forgiveness and love. Finally, Jesus remembers us as he comes into his kingdom; through him we return to our spiritual home with God when our mortal lives end.

Transcendence. Unity. Transformation.

The Apostle Paul gives us a glimpse at how transcendent union with Christ transforms the followers of Jesus. To start, we develop a new relationship with our moral roots, Old Testament law. Instead of feeling condemned by our inability or just plain refusal to keep these rules, the people of God strive to govern themselves by the spirit of moral law as revealed by Christ himself:

> You shall love the Lord your God with all your heart, and with all your soul, and with all your mind, and with all your strength . . . You shall love your neighbor as yourself.
>
> *Mark 12:30,31*

One cannot live according to this great commandment — which in encompassing all others transcends them — without having experienced a conversion of the heart, and in this transformation we, in the spirit of Christ, also fulfill the law. We keep God's law not for the sake of tradition or conformity, or simple obedience, but because in our love, we no longer desire to turn from God, or to hurt others.

What is more, we strive to live in harmony with God's gift to us, the earth. In growing consonance with nature, our attitude transforms from one of fear and exploitation into one of stewardship and nurture. Thus, in the new Adam, we embrace our new Eden and care for it maturely, rather than flee it in alienation, as we did the old.

In this, the unity of God is revealed yet again in Christ, as through the Jews, God's chosen people, comes salvation for all people and for the earth itself. Even as in Yahweh, the transcendent one who cannot be contained by the mind of humanity and whose name cannot be spoken, God's chosen are transformed — and fulfilled. Through the Jews all humanity, all life on earth is invited to bask as one in the divine light of Abraham and Sarah and Jacob.

As ecstatic as these words may seem, the Apostle Paul goes on to set forth even more astounding claims regarding Christ's ministry. For, according to Paul, the Holy Spirit's unifying work in Christ does not end with this invitation to humanity. Rather, the apostle asserts that Jesus goes on to unify *all Creation*.

> [God] has made known to us the mystery of his will, according to his good pleasure that he set forth in Christ, as a plan for the fullness of time, to gather up all things in him, things in heaven and things on earth.
>
> *Ephesians 1:9,10*

This teaching, of the Cosmic Christ, implies that somehow the purpose of the entire universe is not fulfilled until God sends the Christ into it as salvation incarnate. In short, Paul believed that somehow, Christ is the keystone that makes Creation itself whole.

Transcendence. Unity. Transformation.

By his transcendent presence becoming one with the universe, Jesus acts as the divine catalyst that will transform the very cosmos into God's mature realm.

With this notion, however, we denizens of a scientific age finally must protest that Paul has gone too far. Or perhaps more kindly, we acknowledge that Paul wrote at a time when Creation comprised heaven, the firmament, the earth, and sheol, a Hades-like underworld of the dead.

Would Paul and the author of John's gospel have declared the Christ as cosmic had they realized the vastness of the ever-expanding cosmos? Would they have dared suggest that God's presence as a human being on our tiny speck of a planet could fulfill the entire universe with its grand billions of galaxies?

Perhaps.

The remaining chapters of this book will offer a contemporary answer to this question, with a conclusion that may surprise you. In addition to discussing the implications of the Cosmic Christ, the rest of Part II: The Great Awakening, will deal with some of the other difficult issues raised in this chapter that relate to our personal faith.

To wit: If Christ indeed offered his very life to reconcile humanity with God, then how do we share in the benefits of this sacrifice? And a related question: If Jesus fulfills us through his life, death, resurrection and ascension, then why do we remain — no less as Christians — alienated beings? In short, if Christ is the bridge between us, indeed, between all Creation, and fulfillment, how do we go about crossing?

CHAPTER 16

The Divine Physician

We continue our discussion of the new Adam by way of contrast with those original sinners, the old Adam and Eve. We've already noted how, as Adam and Eve eat from the tree of the knowledge of good and evil, they get more than they bargain for; for with this knowledge comes alienation. Yet in a way, they also get less than what they bargain for, because the moral knowledge that they do acquire is limited and often confusing.

Their disappointment has been handed down to us, their children, in at least two ways. First, we find that no mere mortal is wise enough to be the final moral authority. No matter how good our intentions, we miserable sinners can spend hours arguing about such issues as abortion, the death penalty, military spending, air strikes against terrorists and taxing the rich to help the poor, and not come to a consensus about which are the best moral choices. Whatever progress we do make over such issues occurs when we admit that no one's judgment is perfect and that even people of good faith can differ in moral opinion.

This, in turn, reflects the second sense in which our moral knowledge is limited, for we are not wise spiritually, either. Spiritually wise? Simply put, since God alone is good, we can know good only by knowing God, and this will not occur completely until our Maker finishes creating us — redeems us — after this life is over.

In other words, until God's creative hand fulfills us by calling us into the direct presence of Providence forever, we will continue to struggle with moral uncertainty. Moreover, as long as we remain immature spiritual beings, we will continue at times to choose evil even when conscience makes our moral choices clear. When we do indeed make such a choice, we flee fulfillment; when such choices become habit, we weave our shadow about us as a shade against the light of completeness, wholeness, spiritual maturity.

It's like people who turn to the World Wide Web for companionship but only get lonelier the longer they're online, or children who learn to eat for comfort and grow up addicted to junk food. New Testament evangelists used the language of healing to explain the ministry of Jesus Christ. When writers of the Gospels reported that Jesus cured disease, they also were communicating his power to heal the soul.

In fact, it is in his role as healer of body and soul that we can gain a better understanding of why orthodox Christians view the new Adam as the keystone of God's creation of humanity. This brings us to the topic of how physical healing complements God's overall creative process.

During the years that I worked as a magazine editor at the Yale University School of Medicine, I would periodically attend a talk by some eminent physician who would remind the audience that neither doctors nor medicines heal; rather, they only help the body maintain and repair itself. As a Christian, I have come to view the body's natural healing force as the work of God's transforming hand, much as I do the conception and birth of a baby, the healthy development of a child, or a successfully resolved mid-life crisis. I also view old age and even death in this same light, for these too can lead us home to God.

As God sends us the Christ, the divine transforming hand manifests itself in yet another way, and Jesus reveals this by repairing the human body. The New Testament reports that Jesus healed the full spectrum of disease, from blood disorders to deafness, blindness and crippled limbs. Again, it's tempting to view such reports as mere evangelistic ardor. After all, these accounts confront us with the apparent contradiction of a physician healing a patient not gradually, with medicine, or counseling, or physical therapy, but instantly, with a touch or perhaps a sharply delivered command. This runs contrary to all we've ever come to expect from the healing process.

But let us revisit Christ's healing in the context of transcendence, unity and transformation.

In the spirit of our watchwords, I believe that we can discern a paradox that makes sense of its apparent contradictions. A faithful patient approaching the Christ for healing undergoes a transcendent spiritual experience. In this, a paradoxical unity occurs — the soul of the patient and the spirit of Jesus unite — and in this union the person is transformed, body and soul. Fulfillment, wholeness, healing have occurred.

It's important to note that in such healing, Jesus as physician reveals the divine unity in and with all humanity. When the sick person's soul freely engages the transcendent God-with-us in Christ, we catch a brief glimpse of the oneness God will manifest at the End of Days, when Alpha and Omega unveil their unity. For in one's transcendent embrace of the Christ, the soul-in-creation is united with its Source, or Alpha; its Fulfillment, or Omega — and thus is transformed.

In the Gospels, this dynamic reaches a climax when

Jesus brings deceased patients back to life. Of all the contradictions to our everyday experience! Yet again we discover a paradoxical truth overarching the apparent contradiction.

Transcendence. Unity. Transformation.

As the transcendent Christ reaches out to the soul residing in timelessness, the receptive spirit becomes one with God in the unity of Alpha and Omega. In this mystical fusion, body and soul become whole as well, transformed by the healing/creative power of God.

The unity of Alpha and Omega. As autumn faithfully returns each year, we too keep paying homage to Creation's harvest. And like morning to the night, we also reprise the watchwords of paradox.

Now let us bring these concepts together. To better understand Jesus as the healer of soul and body. To embrace Jesus as the healer of humanity and of the single soul.

Note that among Jesus' patients, their alpha and omega reunion brings about a spiritual transformation. The patient's soul is healed by uniting with Jesus, and this is reflected in the patient's body becoming whole. On another level, though, the healing encounter prophesies a larger healing/creation event — God's act of salvation, when the dead are raised at the end of time.

For the culminating transcendence, unity and transformation will occur on the Last Day, when the cosmos itself will move beyond all matter, space, energy and time and return to unity with the Creator. In this, the universe will be transformed, reborn; and the body of everyone who ever lived will be reborn as well, and reunited with its once-departed spirit.

Transcendence. Unity. Transformation.

All souls shall transcend death. People of all times and of all places shall be alive and together as one in the direct presence of our Creator. When we dead awaken, we shall be transformed and united with new bodies like those of the Christ after his resurrection.

The universal reunion. The Cosmic Christ returning in power to judge all of Creation. The grand paradox.

We continue our pursuit.

CHAPTER 17

The Paradox of Salvation

Christ's work as physician also implies his role as liberator, a theme that we will explore in this and the following chapter.

Doctors often say that a healed person is free of disease. Perhaps this sense of liberation is felt most pointedly when one recovers from a life-threatening sickness, or is relieved of the symptoms of a brain injury or serious mental illness, the great robber of our humanity. Notably, the New Testament reports that Christ did not just relieve the symptoms of psychosis as does modern medicine, but actually cured such diseases. New Testament writers understood such healing as rebuking the demons that possess people.

Remember how we earlier had discussed the human soul as a union between mind and spirit? We also took special care not to confuse the involuntary nature of mental illness with the intentional nature of sin. Keeping these caveats in mind, we can view Jesus' healing ministry to the mentally ill as a harbinger of his role as healer of the sin-sick soul in all of us.

Because of our modern ability to treat but not cure psychosis, Jesus' healing of the mentally ill presents us with yet another phenomenon that contradicts both our everyday experience and scientific state of the art. Yet even here I believe that we can detect a paradox that supersedes these apparent contradictions. In fact, I view Jesus' healing of mental disorders as part of the same paradoxical dynamic that was at work with the other illnesses that he healed. Namely,

Transcendence. Unity. Transformation.

In his encounter with a mentally disturbed person, the transcendent spirit of Jesus would embrace the patient's soul. In this experience, a kind of paradoxical unity-in-diversity would occur, as the soul of the ill person reunited with its Source and Fulfillment. In this encounter, the entire person was transformed, becoming whole in mind, body and spirit, in reflection of God's unity.

But what does all this have to do with Christ as a spiritual liberator who overcomes the powers of evil by dying on a cross? There is more to this mystery than you or I can presume to understand. Still, we may be able to grasp something of the cross's healing power should grace and healing on a cosmic scale have anything in common with how we experience these blessings every day.

Wait. The cosmic act of grace revealed in our everyday lives? This may be the central liberating paradox of Jesus' ministry.

To pursue this, let's consider what it takes to help heal our own deep emotional wounds caused, say, by the death of a loved one or perhaps a major career setback. Such events can cast the withering shadow of alienation over us. The paradox of this world seems unbearable. Negative faith taunts us with the apparent absurdity of existence.

"This is what it means to be under the Almighty's protecting wing?" we ask. "Has God forgotten us? Or has God been just a child's imaginary friend all along?" We may even be tempted to give up on life.

When such times arrive, as they do for all of us, who do we turn to for help? Usually someone we can relate to, someone with whom we have something in common. While this may be a parent or sibling, it's even more likely to be a peer who's gone through a similar experience.

In fact, the closer the common experience, the stronger the empathetic, healing bond. Every person who's been helped by a 12-step program such as Alcoholics Anonymous or other support group can testify to what a relief it is that someone else has been through the hell that we've suffered and has survived and moved on — often becoming more mature, more compassionate in the process. We're not alone. There's hope after all, and maybe even meaning beyond all this grief.

I believe that serving as such a peer for each of us is a crucial part of Jesus' mission. Remember back in Part I, when we talked about God as the ultimate empathy? Jesus puts a human face to this aspect of God.

God sends us Jesus, the Word, as a human being not only to bring the transcendent to us, but also to be present with us in our day-to-day lives. Jesus experiences life not from afar, as some detached observer, but directly, as a friend. In the person of Jesus Christ, God comes among us to live the entire range of human experience, from the heights to the depths; to share all the day-to-day rewards and joys and temptations and disappointments and drudgery and boredom that is the human experience.

Every day, and especially during his three-year ministry at the end of his life, Jesus faced the specter of this world's apparent contradictions to his faith, hope and love for God. Jesus' ministry of compassion and forgiveness ran up against lies, selfishness, greed, insanity, sexual wantonness, hypocrisy, cowardice, envy, ignorance, jealousy, stupidity, blasphemy, coldness of heart, not to mention the rage and vengefulness of closed minds.

Jesus' life was marked by acceptance and adoration by some, and hatred and persecution by others. Yet even his disciples betrayed and abandoned him at the time of his crucifixion. He was left alone to face public humiliation and an undeserved, torturous death. Hence, Christ in many ways "paid his dues" as one of us.

Jesus understood firsthand just how painful and alienating human life could be. Thus we can share with him as a friend the painful experiences that we encounter every day. Yet, even with this comforting thought we find ourselves faced with an apparent contradiction to orthodox faith.

For, to the time that he was crucified, there was one brand of human alienation that Jesus himself did not experience: sin and its attendant guilt. Jesus never knew the anguish of treachery that racked his betrayer Judas, leading him to suicide. Nor did Jesus experience the guilt that Peter felt as he heard the crock crow twice. In short, because of his pure and true heart, Jesus did not know what it felt like to be a hypocrite or traitor.

How does this contradict our own faith? Chillingly simple. Jesus' utter lack of guilt raises a seemingly insurmountable problem when we try to regard him either as our best friend — the ultimate in empathy — or as our bridge to God. In short, he's just too perfect.

For perhaps the greatest obstacle facing each of us who strives to serve God is our own sense of sinfulness, of being a traitor. How then can the "Beloved in whom God is well pleased" relate to that sense of unworthiness, guilt and hopelessness that engulfs the rest of us in whom God is not so well pleased?

The Paradox of Salvation

"Thus conscience," the Bard observes, "makes cowards of us all," plunging us ever deeper into alienation, tempting us to lash out at the world in our sinful isolation and withdraw even further from the life to which our Creator invites us. However repentant we may feel, our own history is always there, holding up a mirror. And what do we see? Plenty of bitter evidence that we are unreliable. Hypocritical. Unworthy of God's or anyone's love.

Thus it would seem that there is little hope for our experiencing inner peace either in this life or the next, at least through Jesus. For though the Christ may have been sent to show us by example how to transcend our alienation and its attendant feelings of guilt, shame and unworthiness, he has done nothing to make him feel guilty, shameful or unworthy.

So how can Jesus possibly teach us by example to overcome these obstacles if he's never encountered them directly? Such is the dilemma faced by the holy one of God. And such is the paradox that we will pursue next chapter.

The Divine Liberator

How can Jesus even pretend to show us the way home from the alienation of treachery and hypocrisy — or any other sin for that matter — when he himself never committed such sin? To discover just how, we turn first to Old Testament prophecy and then to New Testament evangelism. For both imply that the faithful Messiah must take on himself the pain and alienation of the world's sin for our sake.

To begin, Isaiah's prophecy of God's suffering servant says that:

> All we like sheep have gone astray;
> we have all turned to our own way,
> and the Lord has laid on him
> the iniquity of us all.
>
> *(Isaiah 53:6)*

Hence, paradoxically, it's not *despite* his utter innocence but *because* of it that Christ receives the chastisement for our wrongdoing. His innocent blood is offered as a sacrifice to God for our sins, as once lambs and other animals were offered in Judaism.

Yet the ritual sacrifice of these animals, whose death was quick and humane so that they would not suffer, was in stark contrast to what the Christ experienced at the hands of his Roman executioners. Often a crucified person did not simply die from trauma or loss of blood. The prisoner slowly asphyxiated, no longer having the strength to hold his head up. In some cases, before suffocation could end a prisoner's misery, the heart would burst; one died literally of a broken heart.

If such torture were not punishment enough for one innocent individual to pay for our sins, Christ's spiritual crucifixion went beyond a horror of physical agony. The Spirit of God within him was tormented as Jesus on the transcendent plain accepted into his heart the guilt and shame and spiritual pain of the human race, past, present and future. Moreover, Jesus accepted this ordeal willingly, without uttering a single curse against us, or Creation, or the God who called him to this most bitter of trials.

What a crushing burden. As biological life ebbed away from Christ on the cross, his spirit descended into the timeless shadow of alienation. Like the brightest star whose life had ever collapsed into a black hole, Christ's soul diminished as it descended into the painful darkness of sin that can engulf every human heart.

During this awful journey, Jesus experienced the same degree of agony as any "soul in prison," including the devil himself. Only, once the intrepid spirit of Jesus did reach the level of Satan's alienation, it did something even more remarkable. The innocent Christ ventured into a realm of darkness beyond which the soul of Satan could ever imagine.

This is the state of non-being perhaps best described as Nadir, the bottom of the black hole of existence. It was here that Jesus' spirit, infinite in love, diminished to less than a single mathematical point, infinitesimal. It is here that we discover that the paradox of this world is a mere pretender to the utter darkness of another paradox: that of ultimate alienation.

For Nadir is true death. The utter absence of God. Non-existence, the dreaded oblivion that the soul fears more than hell itself. Hence, it was never more appropriate for anyone to cry out as Christ did from the cross: "My God, my God, why have you forsaken me!" [Matthew 27:46, Mark 15:34]. For what human being, even the Christ, can bear the loneliness of God?

As Jesus' cry from the cross reverberates in our ears, the contradiction that it implies nearly bursts our hearts. Has the torture of the cross finally caused the Christ — faith incarnate — to lose faith, to capitulate to despair? Has the transcendent given way to the paradox of this world?

No. For Jesus was not forsaken by God on the cross. In fact, paradoxically, God could not have been closer. For it was the almighty presence of Godself that helpless was being crucified.

In awe we approach the foot of the cross to ponder the watchwords, which have never been more sacred.

Transcendence. Unity. Transformation.

For with the Christ's apparent cry of abandonment, the Spirit of God in Jesus paradoxically transcends Nadir by becoming one with nothingness. Yet even in death the Spirit is not destroyed. To the contrary, in this unity, all Creation is transformed.

We see glimmerings of this paradox in the New Testament accounts of the crucifixion. For as weak and exhausted as he is, Jesus signals to us from the cross that he is fulfilling scripture. As he cries for God not to forsake him, Jesus quotes the first line of Psalm 22, a psalm that refers to the suffering servant of God, the Old Testament theme that we had previously discussed.

In this, the divine paradox is reflected as Jesus, the divine servant of humanity, speaks as God's suffering servant:

> My God, my God, why hast thou forsaken me?
>   Why are you so far from
>   helping me, from the
>   words of my groaning?
>   My God, I cry by day but you
>   do not answer;
>   and by night, but find no rest . . .

Psalm 22:1-2

The prophetic psalmist (Psalm 22:6) goes on to describe how the suffering servant is "scorned by others and despised by the people." But then in a stunning display of faith, the psalmist does an abrupt turnaround to make it clear that his message is not one of despair, but of inexplicable, paradoxical hope. For despite his woes, the suffering servant offers a hymn of praise:

> I will tell of your name to my
>   brothers and sisters;
> In the midst of the congregation
>   I will praise you:
> You who fear the Lord, praise him!
>   All you offspring of Jacob,
>   glorify him;
>   stand in awe of him, all you
>   offspring of Israel!
> For he did not despise or abhor
>   the affliction of the afflicted;
> he did not hide his face from me,
>   but heard when I cried to him.

Psalm 22:22-24

Finally, the psalm concludes with the stirring words:

> . . . I shall live for him.
> Posterity will serve him:
>   future generations will be told

about the Lord,
and proclaim his deliverance to a
  people yet unborn,
saying that he has done it.

Psalm 22:29-31

Even as Jesus fulfills the opening words of this psalm by living them, he calls our attention to the psalm's conclusion. By so doing, he communicates that we, like him, must not lose faith, no matter how dark the moment of trial — for in fulfilling the promise of the divine paradox, Christ has brought the light of God to where there could be no light, to oblivion itself.

Transcendence. Unity. Transformation.

Christ transcends time to accept the burden of our sin in the eternal realm of the spirit. In that realm, his innocent soul becomes one with us, engaging in a death embrace with the sinful spirit of humanity. And in that unity humanity endures the unendurable.

From this fateful moment on, the faithful have nothing to fear. In the words of the prophet:

But he was wounded for our transgressions,
    crushed for our iniquities;
upon him was the punishment that made us whole,
    and by his bruises we are healed.

Isaiah 53:5

Transcendence. Unity. Transformation.

In Christ, the death clutch of oblivion has become the embrace of eternal life.

19

The Ascent Into Hell

Following Christ's suffering and death on the cross, other paradoxical, liberating events occur that are key to his ministry and will be the subject of the next few chapters. These events include Jesus' sojourn to hell, resurrection, 40 days with his disciples and finally, ascent into heaven. We also will consider the anticipated culmination of Jesus' ministry, his promised return in power as judge on the Last Day.

Again, these events fly in the face of everyday experience. Only now we're going to take a different tack in trying to make sense of them. We're going to turn to the direction from which the Magi once ventured — the East.

This book opened with a reference to Zen *koans*, pointing out the similar use of paradox in these stories and the *meshalim* attributed to Jesus. But now we will tap the wisdom of the East to help us consider Jesus' ministry directly, especially during and after his time on the cross.

In looking at evolution, creation, the nature of the universe, this book has been trying to adapt Western theology to an essentially Eastern view of the cosmos. For the universe that scientists now describe, ever in the process of growth or decay, is more consonant with an Eastern view rather than a Western one. The classic cosmos of the West is stable — even static — a model dating back to ancient Greece.

This view has God launching physical Creation fully assembled, much like a ship setting out to sail the sea of time. Humanity is fully formed from the start, to live out its drama skittering about the deck; the faithful guided by the light of God's truth. It's the job of the faithful to pass along this truth, making minor cultural adjustments as required throughout history.

By contrast, Eastern religion and philosophy are based on a universe that is fluid and ever-changing, much like the organic model that we have been discussing. This cosmos constantly unfolds, grows, becomes.

It's a model that also allows for eternal truth. Only instead of believing that truth can be set down literally in unalterable laws or scriptures, the faithful use spiritual writings to open themselves to the truth. In this model, both spiritual wisdom and the cosmos itself offer us revelations as history unfolds — while the unchanging heart of truth remains transcendent, beyond verbal understanding. Thus truth must be approached through metaphor.

In summary, the fluid, Eastern model of the universe has proven correct. Now the West must adapt its theology. Many theologians already are hard at the task, and as God's blessing will have it, they have several millennia of compassionate Eastern thought to help guide them through the process.

One of the ancient Eastern teachings that we are going to apply to our Christian pursuit of the divine paradox is that of *samsara*. *Samsara* is the great, ever-turning wheel — or ever-swirling whirlpool — of existence. We will enlist both these images, the two- and the three-dimensional, to deepen our insight into the mission of Jesus after his resurrection.

According to the great wheel analogy, the Christ's spiritual journey begins in heaven before the founding of the universe, when the wheel is at its highest point. The wheel's descent begins with the process of creation, and is revealed to humanity through the prophets, who anticipate his coming, and finally directly when Jesus comes to us conceived as a child. This descent continues with his suffering and humiliation on earth, and culminates during the crucifixion, as Jesus journeys spiritually down, down, beyond the depths of hell to Nadir, oblivion, the lowest point of the wheel.

Here we are confronted by our paradoxical watchwords.

Transcendence. Unity. Transformation.

For at Nadir we encounter a key transitional moment as the great wheel moves from its downward direction to an upward swing.

If we could watch a slow-motion film of an upright, turning wheel, say the water wheel of an old mill, as it reaches its lowest point, we would encounter an apparent contradiction. For at the instant that it reaches Nadir, we would see that the wheel in one sense is heading neither down nor up, yet in another sense it is heading both down and up. On further reflection, we could conclude that neither statement is true and yet in another way that they are both true. Our confusion abates when we take the transcendent view and realize that all these statements are true — even if they apparently contradict each other — for we have observed a paradoxical unity of opposites.

A similar paradox occurs when Jesus attains Nadir on the great wheel of existence. It's important to emphasize that Nadir does not represent Jesus' biological death, the ebbing of bios from his body, but the kind of spiritual death that he experienced on the cross. The great wheel actually begins its upswing as the agonized but triumphant Jesus cries out from the cross, "It is accomplished!" and his body dies.

As the great wheel begins its upward swing, we encounter yet another paradox — and a delightful surprise. For Paul in his letter to the Ephesians (4:9) writes that between the time of Christ's death and resurrection, he "descended to the regions beneath the earth," and I Peter 3:19 tells of Christ's "proclamation to the souls in prison." In reference to such passages, the Apostles Creed states that Christ "descended into hell."

But the great wheel analogy offers us an important new insight. Paradoxically, even as the soul of Jesus descends into hell at the moment of biological death, in another sense, with the upward turn of the great wheel, his soul has actually ascended into hell from the oblivion of Nadir.

Transcendence. Unity. Transformation.

Having overcome his encounter with nothingness, having transcended oblivion itself, the Holy Spirit reverses the Christ's spiritual course. In Jesus' unity with us, humanity's course has also changed — with the death of Jesus, the great wheel of human existence has made its upward turn.

We have been transformed, for paradoxically, with the Christ's unjust demise, humanity's spiritual and moral ascent has begun.

CHAPTER 20

The Paradox of the Whirlwind

> In the beginning was the Word,
> and the Word was with God,
> and the Word was God.
> He was in the beginning with God;
> all things were made through him,
> and without him was not anything
> made that was made.
>
> *John 1:1-3*

We continue with our discussion of Christ's ministry in the context of *samsara*. As the great wheel continues its climb from the Christ's visit to hell, two days after his death, Jesus is resurrected. Then he preaches on the earth for 40 days. Biblical accounts of this period paint a picture that presents us with some curious contradictions, especially in the ways that Jesus behaves sometimes as a physical being, sometimes as purely spiritual.

For some time I had assumed that these apparent discrepancies must have resulted from the Gospel author's drawing on source materials from different oral history accounts, or perhaps that the author had applied some spin to the story so his audience could better relate to it. More recently, though, when I read the post-resurrection account in Luke, I wondered if we may not be able to discern a pattern to the way Jesus' resurrected body is described. We will consider this in the context of *samsara*.

Again, let's begin by outlining the apparent contradiction at hand. When Jesus first appears to the disciples after his resurrection, he is famished and eats fish with them [Luke 21:41,42]. This implies that Jesus has been resurrected in physical form in the same, or at least same type of body that he had before he died. And yet, in apparent contradiction, Jesus also appears and disappears from among his disciples — even moving through solid walls — as if he were pure spirit [Luke 24:28-31].

Where is the paradox that helps us unravel this mystery? We see it in biblical accounts implying that Christ undergoes a transformation during his death and after his resurrection. This would be consistent with the notion of Jesus continuing the evolution that began with his conception, a process that was not halted even by his death.

Transcendence. Unity. Transformation.

For before the disciples' very eyes the Christ may be progressively transcending this world, reflecting his unity with God in his ongoing transformation from the present world into the next.

Hence, paradoxically, we see the union of the two worlds, this one and the transcendent, revealed in a new way in the resurrected Christ. Soon after the resurrection, Jesus' body still requires earthly sustenance. But as time progresses, Christ's body continues to evolve into its transcendent form. Finally, at the end of 40 days, this transition reaches a critical stage at which Jesus enters the realm of pure spirit, what his disciples witness as his ascension into heaven.

Transcendence. Unity. Transformation.

Jesus the human being transcends the physical as Christ the divine Word reveals his unity with God in the direct presence of the Creator at the Ascension. In this union, humanity is transformed, introduced into its new existence.

Although the idea of Jesus' ongoing evolution may at first seem uncomfortable to some Christians, I believe the idea is consonant with such a venerable statement of the faith as the Nicene Creed. As it describes Jesus as the incarnation of God known as the Son, the Christ, the Nicene Creed embraces the Cosmic Christ — who is eternally begotten of the Father. Christ is not simply created by God as a human being and then left to function as an independent entity on earth; rather, in the paradox of the Trinity, the Christ continues to be begotten of God, even as he was before the foundation of the cosmos.

As the epigraph of this chapter implies, this eternal begetting is integral to God's role as Creator. Hence, Christ's time on earth plays a central role in God's creation of the world. In summary, when we consider Jesus' begetting, we should not just focus on his conception as a human being, but attempt — however clumsily we mortals may — to view the entire great wheel of the Christ's being to gain a deeper insight into God's ever-begotten Word.

Hence, the eternal begetting of the Word should continue not only in Jesus' resurrection and 40 days on earth, but also after he ascends into heaven. Returning to *samsara*, Christ's return to heaven may not signify that the great wheel of his being has returned to its highest point, as one might first assume. Rather, the Ascension may represent a point that is only part way — perhaps not even halfway — up the great wheel's heavenward swing.

Christ's ongoing development in heaven would be the spiritual equivalent of his physical body maturing on earth after his birth. To briefly digress, at the time we reach full term as a fetus, we are a fully developed baby, mature in a sense; we actually must leave the protection of our mother's body if we — and she — are to survive. We are born into a world outside the womb, however, in which we are mere infants. Would it not make sense that as Jesus enters the Creator's direct presence as the first spiritually mature human being, he as a heavenly newborn would continue his transformation by growing ever more mature in God's Spirit?

We revisit *samsara* to help us visualize this. Only now we use the alternative way in which *samsara* is thought of. We add the dimension of depth, transforming the great wheel into a great whirlwind.

As such the Christ's conception, his introduction to us from heaven, would represent his spirit entering the vortex of the whirlwind. Descending into this spiritual tornado, the Christ ventures into our world during his life, and while on the cross, beyond, into hell, and beyond still to Nadir. After this lowest culmination, the spirit of Christ begins to ascend — paradoxically with biological death — swirling up, up into hell during the two days of separation from our world, then returning to us for 40 days before transcending this world at the Ascension.

Such movement — the continual flow of a spiral rather than a single, circular turn — implies an unbroken series of deaths and rebirths, cycles within the great whirlwind. These cycles are rich in paradox. For example, during his descent from heaven, even as the Christ dies to his heavenly home, paradoxically he also is conceived of the Virgin Mary. While on the cross, Christ dies in one sense under the weight of our sins, only in another sense to be born victoriously into the afterlife. Such is the transformation wrought by Christ on the cross that paradoxically even entering hell is a triumph, for as Jesus does this, the spiral of existence begins its upward climb.

The Paradox of the Whirlwind

The paradoxes of birth and death continue as the Christ soars farther up the whirlwind. Jesus' dies to hell and death as he is resurrected. Jesus dies to the physical universe even as he is reborn into heaven.

Because of the Christ's unity with humanity, the *samsara* whirlwind also can be thought of as our awakening into divine consciousness. What makes this so exciting is the prospect that the Christ's movement up the spiral of existence continues even after he transcends our world for the next. He continues to awaken, eternally begotten of the Creator, growing into his divine inheritance.

Might this inheritance not include the divine attribute of immanence? Note the richness of the attendant paradox. The further Jesus leaves us by ascending into God's Spirit, the more he returns to us in immanent glory.

Hence, in the divine unity, Jesus fulfills his promise to send us the Holy Spirit even as he ascends into God; to become more present to us even as continues his transcendence; thus in sending us the Holy Spirit, in the divine paradox, the Christ also sends himself. Christ does not wait until the end of the world to return to us. Ever begotten of the Creator, he has been returning to us ever since his death. He returns to us even as I write these words. Even as you read them.

Transcendence. Unity. Transformation.

In the unity of God, Christ continues to transcend his life on earth. Yet even as he does so, he awakens into divine consciousness, into divine immanence, and thus the more present he becomes to us. If we open our hearts to his growing presence, we too are transformed.

We awaken.

The Eye of the Needle

I have formed you, and appointed you
to be a light to all peoples,
a beacon for the nations,
to open the eyes of the blind,
to bring the captives out of prison,
out of the dungeons
where they lie in darkness.

Isaiah 42: 6, 7

Our discussion of Jesus' mission in the light of *samsara* finally leads us to two apparent contradictions that are among the most challenging of Christianity: the savior/judge conundrum and the teaching of the Cosmic Christ. These issues will be considered in this and the following chapter.

As for Christ as universal savior and judge, he is purported to be the savior of all humanity, yet he welcomes into heaven only those whom he judges as ready. All others the Christ bars from paradise and supposedly consigns to spiritual prison.

Who is ready to enter heaven? There's the rub. While many Christians are often quick to say that only God knows, they also tend to believe that the truly faithful of their own stripe are the most likely to be invited. Only with so many different kinds of Christian churches around, not all can be correct.

It almost goes without saying that many Christians are taught that the souls of non-Christians are a lost cause. Even as many Muslims and Hindus consider members of their own religion or sect as the sole inheritors of heaven. There's an old joke about the various religious sects each having to themselves their own little room in heaven to keep them eternally blissful in ignorance. But I digress.

Even if we Christians can resolve the savior/judge conundrum, we must then face the contradiction of the Cosmic Christ. In this role, Jesus, eternally begotten of the Creator, plays an integral role in the creation of the universe itself; as such, we must assume that he serves as the savior/judge of all soulful life, no matter where it has evolved throughout the cosmos.

At first blush, how ridiculous. Given what we know of the size of the universe, is it not the mother of all presumption for Christians — on the scale of the universe, a mere subset of human virus skittering about on a mote of cosmic dust — to make such childish boasts? Is our little Jesus to serve as judge over species who may exist countless light years away in cultures that may be far older and more advanced technologically, morally — in however many ways — than our own?

Can even our steady watchwords rescue these venerable Christian teachings from the sophistication of the contemporary age? Perhaps. But in doing so, Christians will need to let go of some cherished assumptions and embrace new possibilities regarding our relationship to the Christ and to the cosmos.

We begin this part of our journey by turning to yet another story told about Jesus, which evokes one of the more enigmatic images in the Gospels, that of the camel that must pass through a needle's eye. A synopsis follows.

> A well-dressed young man — of great wealth — came to Jesus, saying that he had kept the Commandments since birth. And yet he felt as if something was missing. He asked Jesus what else he must do to inherit eternal life. Christ told him to go and sell all that he had, distribute the proceeds to the poor, and join Jesus and his disciples.
>
> When the young man heard this, he walked away, gravely disappointed that he would have to give up his worldly possessions to follow Christ.
>
> Turning to his disciples, Jesus told them, "It is easier for a camel to pass through the eye of a needle than for a rich man to enter the kingdom of God." Astounded, the disciples asked who then might be saved. Christ replied that for people, such a feat is not possible, but "with God, all things are possible."
>
> *Refer to Matthew 19:16-30, Mark 10:17-31, Luke 18:18-30.*

We may tend to shrug off this story as a warning to people (other than ourselves, of course, because none of us is *truly* wealthy) to share more of their money with the poor. Our self-absolution would ignore, however, that Jesus' disciples evidently took the camel image as a judgment against *them*. And the disciples, who if not poor for their day, had hardly any possessions as compared to most of us today in the developed world.

In fact, if you take Jesus' words literally, they condemn just about everyone but the poorest of the poor and that handful of noble souls who voluntarily join them in poverty. Making things even more difficult, other Bible passages make it clear that even these literally poor, miserable sinners do not get off the hook as souls worthy of salvation of their own accord. With this we've run smack into the savior/judge contradiction, with Jesus, the one who's supposed to rescue everyone, judging people by standards that are too high for anyone to attain.

Don't panic. Again paradox overarches contradiction. To discover just how, though, we must look beyond the story's obvious lesson, about how preoccupation with worldly values distracts us from spiritual life.

Although Jesus invokes the self-contradictory image of a camel passing through a needle's eye, he also leaves the clear impression that God can handily accomplish this feat. Actually we, a contemporary audience, may have a bit of an edge over the disciples in trying to make sense of Jesus' startling image, for as already discussed, scientists say that the universe began as smaller than an atom. Hence, it's hardly a matter of faith for us to accept that God can pass a camel through a needle's eye when the Creator has already passed the cosmos through.

Transcendence. Unity. Transformation.

Transcendence. If, from our transcendent point of view, we know that somehow Christ will bring even selfish, wealthy people into heaven, then there must be hope for other sinners as well. As noted earlier, there are plenty of sinners who are not rich; for that matter, even poverty does not exempt us from alienation and sin.

Unity. Every living being is in the process of being created by God. As part of this process for humanity, God sent his Word to become one with us for our fulfillment. Hence, the Creator intends for each of us to be completed, and hence be reunified with Alpha and Omega in heaven.

Transformation. So even if it takes passing the entire universe through the needle's eye, all soulful beings will have the opportunity to be transformed from alienation and sin into completeness, wholeness, unity with God — for God's love shall accomplish it.

All this sounds very hopeful. While I grant the possibility that given free will, some beings may forever choose to run from their fulfillment in God, I cannot conceive of a being forever choosing to live in suffering when God offers the prospect of everlasting joy.

Still, we are left with the problem that as long as Jesus is to assume the role of judge, the implication is that universal salvation is not part of the equation. After all, the services of a judge are not generally required if no one is guilty. As is our custom when we reach such an impasse, we invoke our faithful watchwords.

Transcendence. Unity. Transformation.

When the transcendent Christ comes to earth as a human being, he becomes one not only with humanity, but also with all life, with all Creation. So in venturing to oblivion on the cross, Christ transforms our understanding of death, which, we had previously assumed, had all Creation helplessly bound; in one way or another, everyone and everything was destined to come to a permanent end.

From our new, transcendent perspective, we now see how the Christ can fulfill the destiny of all Creation in life. To wit:

1. Through his unity with people, the human Christ reveals the destiny of humanity.

2. Through his unity with the cosmos as a physical being, the mortal Christ reveals the destiny of the universe.

3. Through his unity as eternally begotten life with created spiritual beings, the divine Christ reveals the destiny of all souls, no matter where they may reside in the universe.

Here is the most profound transformation linked the mystery of faith. Christ has died, Christ has risen, Christ will come again; so it shall be with all humanity, so it shall be with all life, so it shall be with all Creation.

Jesus' resurrection and ascension reveal the transcendent, universal truth that death is not an end of itself, but a transition in God's ongoing process of Creation, of positive transformation. Although bios or the universe may appear the only true reality, Christ assures us that this is not so, that paradoxically, their death does not halt the divine creative process, but rather, allows this process to be fulfilled.

Hence, as noted in the previous chapter, creation takes place in cycles. At the end of each cycle, death paradoxically becomes a kind of birth, a transition to another stage of development. As for the ascended, ever-begotten Christ and his involvement in divine Creation, we return to where we left off last chapter in our discussion of *samsara*.

One Christian view of this teaching would be that the entire lifespan of our universe is but a single cycle of Creation. As such, the culmination of this cycle, the End of Days, will occur when Christ's growth in God — and thus, his ascending into immanence — is complete. Jesus' movement up the ascending spiral of existence will have been fulfilled, his awakening into divine consciousness complete.

This momentous development will occur at the close of God's sixth day of cosmic creation. God's creative work will have been completed. And it will be time for the Creator to rest, to celebrate the universal Sabbath.

As such, God will recall his immanent Spirit, wholly one with the Christ, from the universe. Obediently, as he did on the cross, the spirit of Christ will answer this call by again spiraling down the whirlwind of existence. Only this time, fully ascended into immanence, he will do so not in suffering, but in power.

With Christ having attained unity with all energy, time, matter and every other constituent of the cosmos, the universe will accompany him to oblivion. In a scenario not considered by any scientific theory that I know of today, at the conclusion of time, the universe will reach the paradoxical juncture of infinity and eternity, and its opposing forces, which now push the cosmic boundary outward at ever increasing velocity, would find themselves paradoxically rushing toward each other at nearly the speed of light. The result would be the cosmos turning in on itself, its very fabric swirling together to create an apocalyptic storm, the Great Whirlwind.

Into the irresistible maw of its vortex, the cosmos would quickly draw itself down, not in billions of years, but in a matter of days, hours, perhaps even seconds, compressed by physical forces of a scale not seen since the Big Bang. Down, down it will be drawn into the mother of all black holes. Even as the divine Alpha and Omega reveal their unity, so would God's creation, the cosmic omega becoming one with its alpha; the cosmos, ending as it began, returning to oblivion.

Transcendence. Unity. Transformation.

Physical creation would diminish, approaching an ultimate unity, transcending itself by returning to God, the ultimate unity; and in this reunion, the universe would be transformed.

Here, beyond the infinitesimal, the cosmos goes out of existence except in the mind of God. Only, paradoxically, by returning to the ultimate existence, at Nadir the cosmos is not destroyed, but fulfilled in God, the true reality. Beyond the infinitesimal, Creation encounters infinity; beyond time, Creation embraces eternity; beyond existence, the dream of Creation becomes real.

These unions of opposites, of nothingness and Reality, of the infinitesimal and the Infinite, the temporal and Eternal, reflect the divine paradox, even as the Alpha and

Omega reveal their oneness at the End of Days. Paradoxically, Nadir will be the pinnacle of *samsara*. The immanent Christ will have been reborn for a final time to culminate this cycle of Creation.

With this rebirth, even as the universe ends and time concludes, all soulful life that ever existed in the concluding cycle of the cosmos will awaken in the direct presence of its Creator. As for those who yearned with all their heart for a home in God, a place in heaven will have been prepared. Christ will harvest them into the loving consciousness of the Holy Spirit that he fully shares with the Creator.

Transcendence. Unity. Transformation.

The camel will have sojourned through the needle's eye. The workers of the vineyard shall receive their wages. In repentance and maturity, prodigal children will come home to their eternal feast.

Through Christ, we and all Creation shall transcend death. With Christ we shall be one with God. In Christ, the Alpha and Omega, we shall be transformed forever.

The Universal Savior

> Indeed, God did not send
> the Son into the world
> to condemn the world,
> but in order that the world
> might be saved.
>
> *John 3:17*

U pon our arrival at Apocalypse Day, we are nearly ready to reconcile the judge/savior paradox and the paradox of the Cosmic Christ. Close though we may be, however, we must first face another difficult question. Namely, what happens to souls who are not brought home by God on Judgment Day? Is there any Gospel message — good news of salvation — that can we offer them?

If there is to be a Final Judgment, it must mean that some souls will not be ready for harvest. As already noted, with no one to judge, Judgment Day is moot. Assuming that there is a Judgment Day, though, how should we approach it?

Should the Third Great Awakening perhaps borrow the view of human destiny described by Jonathan Edwards in 1741? In his famous sermon, "Sinners in the Hands of an

Angry God," Edwards preached that every human being was like an evil spider dangling over the candle of perdition, suspended by a single, silken thread held by the hand of God. Woe to humanity, he thundered at his trembling flock, for "the devil stands ready to fall upon them, and seize them as his own, at what moment God shall permit him."

If Edwards' God seems a terrifyingly capricious, other influential thinkers and artists felt that unharvested souls should move on to eternal punishment that matched the degree of their sinfulness. Reference Dante's *Inferno* and Milton's *Paradise Lost*, or "The Garden of Earthly Delights," the surreal triptych of Hieronymous Bosch. Eternal torment was also chillingly depicted by Michelangelo in the Sistine Chapel and by Rodin in "The Gates of Hell."

As much as I am in awe of these cultural lions, I do not agree with their view of punishment after death. For revenge and eternal torture cannot be the tools of a loving Creator. Nor can I accept the popular, comic book view of hell with horned, cloven-hoofed devils using tridents to goad sullen sinners ever deeper into misery.

At the same time, however, I am not willing write off any possibility of alienation from God in the afterlife. So where do we draw the line? Just what kind of sentence might we sinners face in spiritual prison?

Given the view of Creation that this book has been developing, one would reason that any suffering in the afterlife would be self-inflicted, a result of an individual's abandoning God rather than the other way round. For a crucial subtext of teaching Christ Jesus as Emanuel, God-with-us, is that our souls reflect God within us. God respects us as holy even when we act as anything but.

Then why does God allow us to consign ourselves to spiritual prison? After all, if hell is eternal as tradition has it, what difference does it make whether God punishes us directly in the afterlife or we end up punishing ourselves? Isn't the result the same?

In answer, let's begin by refining our notion of just what hell is. I believe that hell is a the state of being in which what I call "alpha souls" reside after death. Alpha souls?

I believe we're all alpha souls. That is, we're beings who have emerged from the Creator, our Alpha, in conscious life and yet are not mature enough for final reunion with our Creator — our Omega. I do believe, however, that if we set our hearts on serving God in this life, our Creator will grant our heart's desire in the afterlife. We will enter heaven forever fulfilled, as omega souls.

As alpha souls, we are students in the university of life. If we do not dedicate our lives to God, it's as if we have not shown up for classes, ignored the required reading and not even bothered to find out what our assignments were. Come commencement time, we may as well not even show up, because there's no way that we will graduate.

In the afterlife we have no choice but to show up for commencement. We suffer at the ceremony to the degree that we have alienated ourselves from our Creator's love. Only this suffering takes place in timelessness.

To state the paradox in all of this, it is not the Omega, the God outside, that judges us. It is the Alpha, the Christ, the God present in each soul, that acts as judge. So, like Adam and Eve in the Garden, adolescent souls flee from the Creator in the afterlife as they did during life.

Does this leave us with myriad souls being abandoned by God to hopeless, endless self-punishment? I don't believe so. Remember that we are viewing this from our transcendent perspective at the end of time, far beyond the valley of the shadow. From this peak we at last behold the green, liberating pastures of the savior/judge paradox.

From here we recognize that a God who is love does

not stop loving those who flee their own fulfillment, any more than God stopped loving Adam and Eve, or the wealthy father stopped loving the prodigal son. For even a single soul left unfulfilled reveals that the creative work of our Maker is not finished. God the Omega will not abandon God the Alpha, for in divine love, Alpha and Omega are one.

God remains the Creator even after the Last Day harvest is complete. God's Word continues to be begotten. God the Holy Spirit continues its relentless call.

This implies that the rift in God's dominion caused by fleeing, alienated souls will be accompanied by the creation of a new cosmos in another Big Bang. This new universe will begin a new cycle of creation. Having come full circle, *samsara*, the great wheel of existence, will begin to make yet another turn.

Out of the chaos that ushers in this new first day of Creation, God will again begin the long, slow process of creating an ordered universe — so that the seeds of the next spiritual harvest may be sown. As this reborn universe develops, as did its predecessor, the souls who had not been freed from their own darkness will wait, suspended outside of time, for their chance to mature in God's love. In this realm, they will meditate on the lessons of their previous experience, while awaiting rebirth and a fresh chance to struggle toward the light in the new cycle of Creation.

And when the new earth is finally formed and once more gives birth to conscious life, the Christ, the ever-begotten Word, will again come to these reborn souls. Again he will invite them home. Ever begotten in the Spirit, God's Word is ever inviting us home.

Thus, we can make sense of why Jesus would preach in the spiritual prison after his death on the cross. For if the souls there were consigned to eternal damnation, the Christ could offer them no hope. With a cyclical Creation, howev-

CHAPTER 22

The Universal Savior

er, the Cosmic Christ invites souls out of alienation's darkness and into the fulfilling light of God for as long as the cycles of creation continue. For how long? Who knows, perhaps the great wheel turns forever.

Given this scenario, Christ's visit to hell may even mean that souls who repent in the afterlife can be instantly rescued. It would take an extreme, purifying act of faith to recognize the Word's saving presence and reach out to it even in the apparent hopelessness of hell.

Transcendence. Unity. Transformation.

Through such a transcendent, purifying faith, the Alpha and the Omega would reveal their unity. The wounded soul would become whole. Divinely transformed, the newly born heavenly child would find itself basking in God's light forever.

No matter what spiritual state our own alienation may lead us into, in this life or in the next, the Word will be there to guide us home. Because of his experience on the cross, the Christ has ventured beyond the depths of hell. Should our alienation and sinfulness drag us like a millstone down to the depths of Nadir, God's Word will be there to save us if only we call his name.

With such a view of Creation, we are reminded of how heaven and hell, chaos and order, good and evil, suffering and fulfillment — for that matter, all dualities — are transient, and therefore illusory. They are elements of a greater divine plan in which the only true Reality is the unity of Alpha and Omega, God's eternal love.

What then of Satan? How does the fallen angel fare in such a view of heaven and of hell? Satan's murky image becomes hardly less vague, I'm sorry to report.

Perhaps the spiritual prison and its jailer cannot be distinguished any better than heaven and God. This Satan is not so much the individual tempter, or indeed, the fallen angel, but rather like hell itself, an alienated state of being. Satan may embody alienation much as God's Word embodies fulfillment.

We had previously discussed hell as a kind of parody of heaven, and as such, we might expect to find there a demonic unity-in-diversity, a relationship of darkness rather than of light. If heaven is not a place but a state of being, union with the Transcendent, then Satan or hell might represent Legion, union with the illusory shadow.

In addition to its own unity-in-diversity the demonic would reveal its paradox in other ways. To wit, as part of cyclical creation, souls newly emerging into consciousness would ever be falling into the shadow of alienation, even as other alienated souls would ever be emerging from it into God's light. Hence, Satan would find itself in the curiously paradoxical state of ever falling, even as it is ever being redeemed.

At long last, a cyclical Creation also helps us to make sense of Jesus the human being, whose universal mission is that of the Cosmic Christ. We can consider this in two ways, which depend on whether or not earthly life is alone in the universe.

First, in the event that the earth harbors the universe's only conscious life, the love of Jesus helps us to save that life and that of our planet. In this case, the teaching of the Cosmic Christ will offer no contradiction at all. For then the Savior would allow humanity to fulfill its destiny to bring loving, conscious life to other planets, to the galaxy, or perhaps over the millennia, the entire cosmos. In two billion years when the sun has burned itself out and the solar system with it, humanity will be preserved to continue its saga in another star system.

But what if the universe has other planets whose cycles of creation have produced soulful life far different than

The Universal Savior

Homo sapiens? If all the cosmos is indeed awakening to divine consciousness, God may be evolving countless other conscious species. How does the human Christ serve as Emanuel — God-with-us — for all such life?

Like this. No matter what physical form the soul inhabits, no matter where in the universe it evolves, God's continuing care is required for its fulfillment. In every corner of the universe where the Creator evolves conscious life, God must guide immature souls through an adolescent period and back to reunion with God.

Therefore, according to a cosmic pattern, the Holy Spirit becomes one with its species as the Christ, who overcomes death and the devil — and shows its alienated souls the way home to their Creator.

Transcendence. Unity. Transformation.

In this transcendent view of universal life, we open yet another window on the unity-in-diversity of our wondrous Creator God. We discover our divine unity with all mindful life, all kindred souls, that may exist throughout the cosmos. And in this hope, our concept of the universe and our place in it is transformed.

We are not lost in the vastness of the universe, for the Spirit of God fills every aspect of our cosmic home. We are one with all conscious life no matter where it exists. From the time that we shared the same cosmic womb, we and the rest of the universe have been one.

CHAPTER 23

Reunion

John would have prevented him, saying, "I need to be baptized
by you, and do you come to me? But Jesus answered him, "Let
it be so now; for thus it is proper for us in this way to fulfill all
righteousness."

Matthew 3:14,15

Should we choose the path of light, our Creator sup-
ports us in the struggle. To initiate us into the Christ
consciousness and prepare us for the Last Day harvest,
Jesus, our bridge to God, himself has left behind bridges to
guide our growth in the Spirit. Two of these bridges are the
sacraments of Holy Baptism and Holy Communion. Using
the humble elements of water, bread and wine, Jesus leads
Christians in opening themselves to — and involving themselves in — God's creation of themselves.

The first of these sacraments, Holy Baptism, uses
water, an element that God has blessed the earth with in
such abundance that many people take it for granted. But
consider for a moment that life needs water for its very existence. Human beings depend on water so profoundly that
it's a particularly apt symbol of God's Spirit.

Moreover, water has a rich symbolic tradition because
of the role it has played in the history of God's people. We

associate it with the cleansing of sin, for example, because according to the story of Noah, God flooded the earth to rid it of evil. And when God parted the Red Sea to allow the Hebrews to escape Egypt's slavery, water also became a symbol of liberation.

In New Testament times, John the Baptist called on this cleansing tradition when he preached repentance through baptism, so that God could free his followers from sin. He also made it clear, though, that baptism as a means for receiving the Spirit would have to wait for the Holy One of God:

> The one who is more powerful than I is coming after me; I am not worthy to stoop down and untie his sandals. I have baptized you with water; but he will baptize you with the Holy Spirit.

> *Mark 1: 7,8*

Nevertheless, Jesus, despite his spiritual authority, insisted that he be baptized at the hands of John the Baptist. I can think of three reasons for this. First, because this sacrament serves as a bridge between God and humanity, it seems only appropriate that both the Holy One and an ordinary human being be involved in its institution.

Second, because John the Baptist claims no special virtue, it becomes clear from the start that this sacrament's benefits come from God, and not from the human being who pours its water. Third, Jesus submits to John's baptism as an act of humility, to teach us the proper spirit in which to enter our own baptism.

Scripture [Matthew 3:13-17, Mark 1:9-11, Luke 3:21, 22] reports that John's baptism of Jesus was far different from any the Baptist had undertaken before. As he baptized Jesus in the cold water of the Jordan River, the heavens opened, and the Holy Spirit descended in the form of a dove to alight on Jesus. And God's voice said, "This is my beloved Son, in whom I am well pleased."

Transcendence. Unity. Transformation.

The transcendence of Jesus' baptism is revealed as Creator, Word and Holy Spirit make their presence known together. In this revelation of divine unity comes a transformation that is so central to Jesus' ministry that we allude to it every time we call him "Christ."

Recall that this title descends from the Greek *Christos*, a translation of the Hebrew "Messiah," or "the Lord's Anointed." In the Jewish heritage, anointing, or pouring oil over the head, bestows authority and responsibility in the name of God. In the waters of Holy Baptism, Christ is anointed by and receives his commission from the Creator in person, through the Holy Spirit.

From the time of Jesus' baptism, anyone who is baptized willingly in his name also is commissioned into God's service. At our baptism, we (or those who stand up for us as infants) admit our incompleteness in the face of our perfect Creator. We ask God's blessing to enter divine service, and so that we may be made whole. When we make this commitment, something wonderful happens.

Jesus shares his baptism with us. Because we have followed his humble example, the Christ sends us the same Holy Spirit that was bestowed on him at his own baptism. Because we share in both the anointing and the ministry of the Christ, we even take his royal title — in our baptism, we become Christians.

Transcendence. Unity. Transformation.

Through this transcendent, sacramental sharing, we enter the unity of God that was expressed at Jesus' baptism, and in this we are transformed. The soul, the Alpha, the living spirit that God began within us, becomes one with its fulfillment, the Omega, the God who waits outside us. In this Alpha and Omega reunion, we are spiritually reborn in oneness with the perfect soul of Christ and prepare our own souls for an eternity of divine enlightenment.

In summary, *through Jesus*, we enter into a special relationship with God in baptism. In the unity of the Holy Spirit, we are baptized *with the Christ*. Thus, we die to our old, alienated selves and begin a new life *in God's Word*, who enlightens us through the Holy Spirit, the living water that satisfies our eternal thirst for God.

Note how this development reflects an evolution of the Western tradition. From the waters of judgment loosed against the Hebrews and all humanity by an angry God in the story of Noah; to the protector and liberator of Israel at the time of the Passover; to an invitation for all people to ascend into the Spirit of God. Through the eternal cycles of water and the Spirit, our religious tradition is awakening.

CHAPTER 24

Rebirth

You have made us for Yourself
so that our hearts are restless
until they rest in You.

Augustine, Confessions

Though our souls are reborn in Holy Baptism, spiritual growth does not end here any more than physical growth ends when we leave our mother's womb. In Holy Baptism we invite God to create us from within, but the forging of our souls — like the Christ's *samsara* journey, like the Holy Spirit's work throughout all Creation — also follows a cyclical pattern of birth, death and rebirth.

The Eastern Orthodox Church celebrates this in its rich liturgical imagery of rain falling from the sky to sustain life only to return to the heavens to begin the cycle again. So we too go through cycles of life and death in our life in God after baptism. Although baptism allows us to begin life anew, growing in the Spirit means that we will ever encounter new challenges to our faith.

Sometimes these challenges defeat us as we respond in a sinful, faithless way. We may refuse to turn to God for help, or feel incapable of doing so. Or perhaps we just find gratification in the sin. Whatever the case, we flee into the shadow of alienation; in effect, we die to our faith.

When such failures wound our conscience, we feel flawed and hypocritical. We may even feel as if we're living proof of the paradox of this world, and in a way we are. How fruitless it may seem to try living a life that is faithful to God.

But all who make such judgments, whether about their own sins or about others', have not wholly accepted the message of Christ. Mother Teresa sagely observed that Jesus does not call us to succeed, but to be faithful; bearing the cross of our own flawed nature is central to our commitment of faith. Our strength is Jesus, who forgives us and invites us to continue our struggle through the cycles of spiritual life and death in our journey toward the light.

Transcendence. Unity. Transformation.

Every time we stumble and fall and repent of our failure, we reopen our hearts to our Creator's love. In the promise of our baptism, Jesus sends us the Holy Spirit and our spirit is reunited with God in forgiveness. With this reunion, the Holy Spirit completes another cycle in our spiritual life. Thus transformed, we leave our old, dead selves behind and are reborn.

As long as we prodigal children struggle to follow God, our souls will go through such cycles. They are part of the work and birth pangs of the Adam and Eve tale; they are the cross that Christ says we must pick up every day if we are to follow him.

Through the cycles of spiritual growth we learn humility, realizing ever more profoundly our need for God to finish the divine creative process at work within us. We also gain wisdom, as we come to know Satan's wiles in exploiting our incompleteness. Hence, we come to rely on our Creator all the more, and in so doing move further along the path to fulfillment.

CHAPTER 24

Rebirth

Transcendence. Unity. Transformation.

Having entered the life of the transcendent Christ, through the cycles of life and death in the faith we grow in unity with Jesus, and thus in Christ consciousness. So in Jesus we are constantly being reborn. In these transforming cycles of birth, death and resurrection, God creates us, drawing us with Christ our master up the ascending spiral.

Manna

To sustain us on our way toward spiritual maturity, Jesus left for us another sacrament, Holy Communion. As if to remind us that the way of spiritual growth can be difficult, painful, even dangerous, Christ initiated this ritual on the very night that his disciple Judas Iscariot betrayed him to an undeserved, torturous death.

As he shared the Passover supper with his friends, records the book of Matthew (26: 26-29):

> Jesus took bread, and having said the blessing he broke it and gave it to the disciples with the words: "Take this and eat; this is my body." Then he took the cup, and having offered thanks to God he gave it to them with the words: "Drink from it, all of you. For this is my blood, the blood of the covenant, shed for many for the forgiveness of sins. I tell you, never again shall I drink from the fruit of the vine until that day when I drink it new with you in the kingdom of my Father."

It should come as no surprise that over the centuries Christianity's critics have focused on the apparent contradiction that this sacrament presents. On one hand, Christianity begins as a kind of high-minded reform movement of Judaism of two millennia ago. On the other hand, one of

Christianity's sacraments seems to evoke the cannibalism of Paleolithic religion.

But there is a paradox that transcends this apparent contradiction.

Transcendence. Unity. Transformation.

Rather than taking us back to the practice of literally devouring a dead person's flesh and blood, this meal uses bread and wine as a sacramental means for us to awaken into the living spiritual life of the Christ, thus transcending the flesh and blood of the temporal world. In Holy Communion we unite with the risen Christ and are transformed as part of his eternally begotten life.

As the bread and wine nourish our physical bodies, our souls are fortified by spiritual food and drink. As Joseph Campbell points out, in Holy Communion we "eat God" to feed our souls; as this draws us into the life of the Spirit, paradoxically, we also "feed" our Creator.

Such devouring images may seem less shocking once we consider the elements of communion in the context of the ancient symbolic heritage they share with baptism. Like water, wine and bread also play important roles in the Old Testament liberation tradition. For the feast of unleavened bread, from which communion stems, commemorates the Passover, which led to Israel's freedom after centuries of bondage.

At the time of the Passover, God, to compel Pharaoh to free the Hebrews, commanded Moses to have Jewish families smear the blood of a sacrificed lamb over their doorways. This, as the Creator promised, made the approaching angel of death pass safely over their homes, even as the firstborn of unmarked families died. Hence, the Passover wine recalls how the blood of the sacrificial lamb saved the Hebrews from death and ultimately led to their freedom.

Because Pharaoh's firstborn died under the shadow of the passing angel, in his grief he agreed to free the Hebrews. But he gave them so little time to leave that they had to bake the bread for their journey before the dough had a chance to rise. So the unleavened Passover bread also recalls the liberation of God's people and the haste they took to embrace their freedom.

After Pharaoh vengefully broke his promise and sent his army to pursue the Hebrews, God had Moses part the waters of the Red Sea. The Jews escaped to the opposite shore, and God saved them by closing the sea and drowning the Egyptian army. But God's assistance to his chosen people did not end with this miraculous escape. Long after the Hebrews left captivity behind them, God sustained his people in the wilderness with manna, bread from heaven, and with water that sprang from a rock that Moses struck with his staff. Thus, the Old Testament heritage of God's care, nurture and sustenance also is honored in the elements of communion and baptism.

How does our Creator employ communion to lead Christians through the cycles of spiritual growth initiated in baptism? The answer should come as no surprise.

Transcendence. Unity. Transformation.

When we approach the communion table in repentance, we transcend our old lives, which have grown jaded and weary in our struggle to fight Satan using our own limited powers. Then, as in our baptism, we become one with the Christ and are transformed — forgiven of all wrongdoing, refreshed in spirit, we are reborn in God.

In these cycles of death and rebirth, our souls do not simply run in place like a hamster on a treadmill. Rather, through the cycles prodigal children gain invaluable experience, which God uses to usher us along the ascending spiral of consciousness, and thus awaken us in the Spirit. We see this reflected in the sacramental elements as well, only instead of looking to their Old Testament tradition, we turn to their relationship in nature.

For example, note the relationship of water, the element of baptism, to communion's elements of bread and wine. Water induces seeds of wheat and grapes to die to their old forms so they can be reborn to put down roots and bask as mature plants in the sun. In the end, with the sustenance of water, humble, tiny seeds produce abundant crops for the harvest.

Just as water begins a chain of transformation that results in wheat and grapes — and ultimately the products of bread and wine — the Holy Spirit's presence in the waters of baptism initiates a cycle that transforms the soul and readies it for the Last Day harvest and beyond. Through the unity of the Holy Spirit introduced to us at baptism and sustained in communion, the Spirit of Christ grows in us, as we, paradoxically, grow in Christ. This process culminates after biological death, when at the Last Day, our spirits are reawakened at the Great Harvest to be transformed into perfect, everlasting bodies, like that of the risen Lord, and we are welcomed into heaven.

Transcendence. Unity. Transformation.

Christ becomes the Christian's Passover lamb. Through his body and blood we transcend death. In the unity of the Holy Spirit in communion, as in baptism, our souls transform, joining the light of Christ, becoming the light of our Creator.

Through the sacraments we cross the bridge of Christ to our final stage of evolutionary development. Our biological life achieves its ultimate transformation, fulfillment and maturity in Christ. In this the Creator achieves the seemingly impossible; paradoxically, we become part of the eternally begotten life of God, the divine life that cannot be created.

This explains our celebration of the sacraments, which paradoxically are also penitential rites. For, every time we die to our old selves through the sacraments, we experience the unity of God as the soul, emergent from God, our Alpha, becomes one with its fulfillment, God, our Omega.

Transcendence. Unity. Transformation.

In this transcendent union we enter into the divine paradox of the End of Days, when Alpha and Omega reveal their unity. Thus we are transformed. We are awakened in the Spirit, reborn to eat and drink with Christ at God's table forever.

CHAPTER 26

The Universal Soul

. . . so that the just requirement of the law might be fulfilled in
us, who walk not according to the flesh but according to the
Spirit.

Romans 8:4

B
aptism and communion can revolutionize our own
awakening in Christ. They can help the Church work
as one body of Christ in the Third Great Awakening.
They can open the gates to the thousand years of peace.

For all this to happen, though, Christians must receive
the sacraments with an intentional faith. We must stop wast-
ing our spiritual lives by receiving communion thoughtlessly, as if it were an empty ritual. Our time has come to bear
good fruit for the harvest — to translate faith into action.

In these final chapters, we will consider some of the
actions that testify to and nurture our faith. We will discuss
how, in unity with the transcendent Christ, we are transformed from persons who require the external restraint of a
written code, complete with punishments to enforce a standard of behavior, into an enlightened people who have the
law of God "written on our hearts." In short, we will discuss
how the lifelong process of opening our hearts to God
depends on developing spiritual discipline.

Recall that in baptism, each life in Christ begins with humility and a commitment to serve. Yet, even as we are called to such disciplines by faith, our faith, too, is nurtured by them and by other disciplines as well, such as prayer, fasting, reading the Bible and worshipping together. Thus we grow in God's Word and ascend the *samsara* spiral; thus we grow in Christ consciousness.

Such growth, however, must never be considered some pursuit of an esoteric knowledge that removes us or makes us superior to others. To the contrary, as we grow in the immanence of God's Word, we become ever more *connected* with others and with all life. Hence, the first fruits of our faith are empathy and compassion.

I believe that the very foundation of faith-in-action is a discipline that tends to be so quiet that we may be tempted not to think of it as active at all. That unassuming and yet powerful activity is prayer. In a faithful prayer, as in the sacraments, we discover yet another catalyst for transformation as the soul, the spirit emerging, encounters its source, the Spirit fulfilled.

Prayer provides a mirror to the soul that can help our faith mature. If for example our prayers are constantly centered on ourselves and our own needs, the mirror reveals self-absorption and spiritual stagnation. Do we pray to manipulate God or others to serve us? Do we ask for worldly riches and adulation?

Foolish, foolish heart, do not ask God to prove divine love by lavishing wealth on you and the false affections that money or fame may bring. In Christ, we already are assured that God loves us more profoundly than we can imagine. Rather, pray God to send us all the Holy Spirit so that our deeds leave no doubt as to how deep our gratitude is.

The Rev. Thomas Keating of St. Benedict's Monastery in Snowmass, Colorado, likens prayer to an intimate conversation:

> When we begin to pray, it's the beginning of a movement to a deeper union with Christ. Conversation deepens the relationship in all our human relationships. . . [We] move beyond conversation to communion.

Father Keating's reference to conversation means that we not only speak to God, but listen. He teaches a form of meditative prayer called centering prayer in which one spends 20 minutes a day, twice a day, focusing on a sacred word, such as God or Jesus, silence, mercy, or the like as a way of inviting the Holy Spirit into one's heart. Such prayer complements the Third Great Awakening in that it draws both on ancient Christian tradition and Zen centering meditation, in which one enters a peace that transcends verbal understanding.

As God speaks to us in the silence of our hearts, we grow in the Spirit. Our prayerful reply reflects our divine relationship of love and faith: As we grow in love, we share with God our concerns about ourselves and others, for the stewardship of the earth; as we grow in faith, we ask that our Creator's will be done.

Transcendence. Unity. Transformation.

In the transcendent act of prayer, Christians become one with Christ. In this unity we are transformed. We cross the paradoxical bridge between meditation and action: We obey Christ's command to "pray without ceasing" when our divine friendship becomes present in how we live our lives.

In the Western tradition, such prayer life grows out of the Jewish tradition of *halakah*. According to this way of life, as explained by Eric Fromm, we

> must act not only according to general principles of justice, truth, and love.

Rather, every act of life is

> 'sanctified,' becoming imbued with a religious spirit.

Christians encounter sacred presence in their lives through their relationship with Jesus, as the Rev. Jay Rochelle states simply but powerfully:

> Jesus did not teach a way of life; he *is* a way of life; he is *the* life.

At the dawn of the Third Great Awakening, Christians must become that life through the divine leavening of the sacraments and prayer. As we grow in the Cosmic Christ, our lives should come to reflect a consonance, a harmony, between our souls and the very life of the universe. As the risen Christ awakens into God's immanence, we too awaken into a new, positive relationship with other people, with all life, with all Creation.

Transcendence. Unity. Transformation.

In our growing, transcendent union with the Cosmic Christ, we experience yet another wondrous transformation. For as we transcend our narrow, ego-centered view of self-interest, the apparent contradictions of self-interest and of universal compassion reveal their paradoxical unity.

In other words, what is good for the life of the community, of the earth — God's dominion — is good for us individually. Because we are connected with others, we share in their pain and in their blessings. In awakening to God and the life of Creation, we in fact awaken to our true selves, our transcendent, eternal selves. And in this, we are transformed.

We become one with the love of God.

CHAPTER 27

The Discipline of Love

Whoever welcomes this child
in my name welcomes me;
and whoever welcomes me
welcomes the one who sent me;
for the least among all of you
is the greatest.

Luke 9:48

As we near the conclusion of this book, we reconsider the shocking amount of power God puts in our hands by creating us as free, conscious beings. Modern technology has wrought a Dickensian paradox in which we live in both the best and the worst of times. Even as our ability to make maps advances — whether of the human genome or the universe — our course as the human race seems increasingly obscure. Violent civil, religious and international conflict ushers us out of a century whose 160 million dead from war and genocide, in the words of Professor Walter Reich, former director of the United States Holocaust Memorial Museum, has "mangled . . . the confidence the world once had in the possibility of human progress."

Every year, technology advances the life-and-death power that we hold over ourselves and our living planet. We need a Great Awakening of our religious and spiritual traditions to temper this explosion of knowledge with wisdom. Together — scientist and non-scientist, cleric and laity — we must awaken into the discipline of love.

Love, a discipline?

Every loving relationship involves a choice to give up something for the sake of something else. By way of example, a romantic relationship or marriage requires conscious effort every day. Even as one partner must struggle, say, against reflexive, angry behaviors learned as a child, the other may have to battle the wandering eye.

Human beings are related to one another and to all life on earth. To make this a loving relationship, we must be intentional. We too must make sacrifices.

Transcendence. Unity. Transformation.

To love, we offer a sacrifice: we transcend our selves. Love celebrates the unity of God that exists between us and others, between us and all life, between us and the earth. Embracing this unity transforms us forever; paradoxically, in transcending our selves, we awaken to our true selves.

For Christians, God sets an example of loving discipline in many ways. Our Creator sacrifices some divine power — the control over our will — so that we may live freely as conscious beings. Our savior, Jesus, embodies this discipline even to sacrificing his life. God's Spirit empowers us with love to awaken us.

This affects the way Christians live their lives, writes Roman Catholic scholar John P. Meier, as Christ awakens us to:

> . . . mercy without measure, love without limits — even love of one's enemies. To many of us, such ideals, however noble, seem simply unattainable. To Jesus, they were possible, but only for those who had experienced through Him God's incredible love

174

changing their lives. Radical demand flowed from radical grace. If religion was grace, then ethics was gratitude — and not just for the interim.

Hence, Christians' enter the Great Awakening in thankfulness. We begin to understand how in God's grace, we too can fulfill God's law in the Spirit of Christ. This is a prescription for radical, positive change.

The Great Awakening is particularly important to Christians who have been taught that God imposes on us a discipline of fear. Too often such teaching has an unintended effect; people end up feeling coerced, as if God or the Church were violating their freedom and autonomy. In response, they may rebel with highly unloving behavior.

Perhaps the best way to contrast the disciplines of fear and love is in light of the Ten Commandments, the foundation of Western morality and ethics. In the discipline of fear, we approach the commandments as rules that circumscribe our behavior on pain of punishment in this world and the next; "The Great Thou Shalt Nots" a rebellious young friend of mine once called them. I wish I could speak with her again today to suggest how, in the Great Awakening, our perception of the commandments becomes quite positive, even liberating.

To start, the first three commandments deal with our direct relationship with God. God should be our only god; we should not take the holy name in vain; we should honor the holy Sabbath. In the spirit of Great Awakening, how do we perceive these commandments?

If we truly are grateful for the Spirit inviting us into the Christ consciousness and creating us in the divine image, then God is paramount in our hearts. We eagerly take a sabbatical day to say thanks in fellowship and song and prayer; our loving community restores our soul, reaffirming that we are the body of Christ. With God as our best friend, we would never think of using the holy name as a casual curse word or swearing falsely by it.

The last seven commandments deal with our relationship to others. We honor our parents and the fidelity of marriage. We don't murder or steal or be envious of our neighbor's goods or whatever other gifts God may have provided our neighbor.

In the Great Awakening, we fulfill these commandments in our hearts, by loving our neighbor as ourselves. Awakening in Christ, we are ever more grateful for the gift of life. Awakening in the Spirit who is empathy itself, we awaken into compassion.

If we can awaken even to love our enemies and truly believe that it is more blessed to give than to receive, then must we be commanded not to steal from or be envious of our neighbor? Must we be commanded on pain of eternal punishment not to break our vows of marriage, or cause others whom we love to violate theirs?

No, but we must be lovingly reminded. Even if we awaken in Christ, it is all too easy to stagnate or stray and then, in denial, convince ourselves that we are doing just fine. The Commandments offer us an ethical standard, and if we don't measure up, we should take a long, careful look to discover where we've gone wrong.

In Christ, we have a friend who is always there to guide us home when we prodigals decide to return. Christ does not command us to obey or die. He calls us to walk with him and live.

In some ways, such grace may make it seem as if Christians are getting let off too easily. We can always come home when we're ready. In other ways, though, fulfilling the spirit of the law actually may be more difficult than keeping its letter.

Take, for example, Christ's exhortation to love our neighbor. To keep the spirit of this Commandment today, we must also be good stewards of the Earth. When we remove ourselves from spiritual communion with our environment by poisoning the atmosphere and thoughtlessly destroying natural habitats, driving other species to extinction, we exhibit not the love of God but the alienation of the destroyer. Christ calls us to be God's presence on earth, just as he was.

This charge may seem maddeningly impossible. For in apparent contradiction, Jesus not only calls us to perfection, but also says that his yoke is easy, his burden light. How can we, the humble seed of the field, aspire to the maturity of wheat and grape, let alone sacramental bread or wine? Of our own power we cannot, anymore than a seed can will itself to grow.

Transcendence. Unity. Transformation.

Transcending our own will, we thus awaken, trusting in God, making ourselves vulnerable to the one who made himself vulnerable to us. We thus awaken, uniting with God, opening the harvest of our hearts to the Spirit's pinch of yeast. We thus awaken, inviting our Creator in to leaven our hearts, our lives, our souls.

Leaven our hearts, oh Jesus, as we open them to the Spirit's wisdom in prayer. Leaven our souls in the sacraments as we share in your death — so that we may also share in your eternal life. Leaven our lives, dear Jesus, that we may share your light with others and open ourselves to all Creation.

Hence, in the discipline of love, we can test whether our faith is alive. For as Jesus grows in the Creator, returning to us in immanence, he awakens us to all people, all life, all awakening Creation. And in sharing our hearts with each other, we awaken further in Jesus.

Transcendence. Unity. Transformation.

Our pursuit of the divine paradox has led us back to God's unity in diversity, with which we began. Our love of the One becomes real in our love for the One-in-each and the One-in-all. In the unity of Alpha and Omega, we are transformed and fulfilled in compassion.

In love, we awaken.

C H A P T E R

Unity in Diversity

> A good tree cannot bear bad fruit,
> nor can a bad tree bear good fruit . . .
> Thus you will know them by their fruits.
>
> *Matthew 7:18,20*

In the unity of Alpha and Omega, let us end as we began, by considering the Holy Spirit's work both in Christianity and in other religious traditions. Our pursuit of the divine paradox has led us to the Cosmic Christ; does the Cosmic Christ, in turn, open the door to the Third Great Awakening and to Christianity's Third Age?

I believe that he does. For by considering a theology of creation based on a cosmos that is not static but in process, we encounter a Christ who, as God's ever-begotten presence, has come to God's people in three ways:

1. In anticipation of the Christ
2. In the person of Jesus Christ
3. In the Spirit, as the ascending Christ.

We have come to know Jesus as the human expression of the Cosmic Christ who in his continuing role in God's ongoing act of Creation, unites us in Spirit even with soulful beings throughout the universe, should they exist.

179

If we can accept that the Cosmic Christ reigns even across the galaxies, then why can we not accept that he can unite a single species on one planet? I make a paradoxical point here. I believe that in the Spirit, Christ has indeed been working ceaselessly toward such harmony here on earth; it's simply time that we Christians moved beyond our stubborn resistance to the idea that the Spirit moves through other traditions as well as our own. In short, let us Christians pursue the divine paradox hand-in-hand with our sisters and brothers of other traditions.

Transcendence. Unity. Transformation.

Let us transcend race, gender and sexual orientation, and embrace our unity as God's children. Let us transcend sect and denomination and discover our kinship as the community of faith. Let us transcend our flat-earth view with the transcendent vantage point of the space pioneer, the nexus of spiritual inspiration and scientific knowledge.

From this transcendent view, we come to understand our planet as one Garden of Eden. From here our historic, irrevocable choice crystallizes before us: either we rescue this holy gift or in the tragic tradition of Adam and Eve disobey our Creator and destroy it.

Christians may enter into this Third Age maturity keeping in mind what Jesus taught in the epigraph of this chapter. How best do we perceive the work of the Spirit? Neither by the quality of moral proclamation, nor by the height of doctrinal walls, nor by the subtlety of our pretensions. Rather, the Spirit reveals itself in the fruit of our compassion.

In his own ministry, Jesus did not condition his love on whether the person in need was like himself, a Jew; even as Jesus raised his Jewish Lazarus from the dead, he also forgave the Samaritan woman at the well and even called on God to forgive the pagan soldiers who nailed him to the cross.

Following this example, Christians should build bridges to people of other religions, beginning with Judaism, our parent faith, and moving onto other faiths within the Western tradition. To wit, should we not acknowledge the work of the Spirit in Mohammed, at whose teaching hundreds of millions of people throughout the world strive to live honest, compassionate lives? Is it not the power of God that inspires countless millions to bow their faces to the ground in prayer each day?

As for Eastern traditions, may we not also acknowledge the Spirit's voice in the compassion, self-control and yearning for transcendence taught by the Buddha and the Dalai Lama of Tibet? Should we not recognize the thousands of Buddhist monks and nuns who have forsaken all worldly concerns to prepare for eternity, and the millions of lay Buddhists who strive for empathy and compassion?

This book has spoken about the shared tradition of *halakah* between Jews, Christians and Moslems, the ideal of having the Spirit suffuse every aspect of one's life. Should we of the West not also consider the *halakah* tradition revealed in the words of Muktanand, a Hindu devotional poet (1761-1830):

> I shall think myself blessed only when I see Him
> in every one of my daily acts;
> Verily, He is the thread
> which supports Muktanand's life.

Christians can discover further kinship with Hindus in discussing faith and science. To accept evolution as God's act of creation, as this book has done, is to embrace scientific discovery as another way that God speaks to us. If so, then the Creator has revealed fundamental insights through the Hindu tradition.

To give a notable example, a cornerstone of modern mathematics — the number zero — was described by the

181

Hindu mathematician and philosopher Sridhara in the year 1000. Zero makes possible modern engineering, physics, and other such disciplines. Hence, the scientific advances of the current millennial age are deeply indebted to the Hindu tradition.

My own acceptance of Hinduism as a faith complementary to Western tradition had to overcome the religion's plural expression of the Deity and its seeming idolatry. How could I, a follower of Christ, relate to religious symbols such as Shiva, divine dancer with many arms, and Genesha, the jolly blue god with the head of an elephant? Helping me to bridge this divide are the writings of Mohandas Gandhi, a Hindu commonly referred to as Mahatma, the Hindi word for "great soul."

Gandhi's autobiography reveals how comfortably the Mahatma refers to God in the singular, which implies that he himself had transcended this difference between the Eastern and Western traditions. In his 1982 film, *Gandhi*, director Richard Attenborough memorably depicts the Mahatma's devotion to religious tolerance as Gandhi, played by Ben Kingsley, shouts in exasperation at his followers who were engaged in murderous sectarian fighting among themselves, "I am a Muslim! I am Hindu! I am Christian! I am a Jew! And so are all of you."

As for the apparent idolatry of Hinduism, it is instructive for Christians to walk in a Hindu's shoes briefly to learn how some of our Western depictions of the divine might appear. In his autobiography, Gandhi reports that he experienced great spiritual peace when in 1890 he made his first visit to a Christian church, the Cathedral of Notre Dame, in Paris. He initially felt discomfited, though, at the sight of people praying at a marble statue of the Virgin Mary — a gesture that seemed like idol worship. But as he observed the devotion expressed on the faces of the supplicants, the

Mahatma recalls:

> they worshipped not stone, but the divinity of which it was
> symbolic . . . by this worship they were not detracting from but
> increasing the glory of God.

What is more, if we are to consider others' beliefs according to their fruits, what better evidence of *halakah* could we discover than the life of Gandhi? Eschewing worldly wealth and status, willing to fast to death for freedom and to unite the people of India in peace, he became perhaps the greatest civil rights leader of the passing century.

Gandhi's practice of *Satyagraha* (*satya* = true; *agraha* = firmness) — nonviolent civil disobedience to achieve social justice — began with *ahimsa*, the teaching not to kill as taught in Buddhism and in the Hindu *Bhagavad-Gita*. But this harbinger of Third Age tolerance also notes that *Satyagraha* was strongly influenced by Christ's Sermon on the Mount, especially the verses:

> But I say to you, Do not resist an evildoer. But if anyone
> strikes you on the right cheek, turn the other also; and if any-
> one wants to sue you and take your coat, give your cloak as
> well.
>
> *Matthew 5:39,40*

Gandhi read this not as encouraging passive acceptance of abuse, but rather as a nonviolent commitment to moral principle even in the face of violence.

Gandhi paid a high price for his religious tolerance. He was murdered in 1948 by a Hindu extremist. Yet in death the Mahatma to this day embodies Great Awakening ideals of nonviolence, religious tolerance and social justice.

We see Gandhi's legacy continue in the Rev. Martin Luther King Jr., a Baptist in the United States, who modeled his civil rights leadership on the Mahatma's example. The

Rev. William Sloane Coffin, Jr., a New England Congregationalist, and other spiritual leaders of the peace movement in the United States in the 1960s and 1970s also followed in Gandhi's footsteps of nonviolent civil disobedience. Gandhi's example also helped to inspire the democracy movements in South America and in contemporary South Africa.

Nonviolent civil disobedience helped to overthrow a dictatorship in the Philippines in the 1980s, and under the moral leadership of Pope John Paul II, helped to bring down the Communist empire of Eastern Europe. In these movements, it was as if the righteous, prophetic power of the Spirit had come full circle, being gifted back to Christians and all who struggled for justice and peace via the gentle, courageous vision of Mahatma Gandhi. Christ, Gandhi, King and the many other martyrs for freedom: in the Spirit, their deaths paradoxically have furthered the life of justice and the fulfillment of all God's people.

Other harbingers of the Third Great Awakening include Thomas Merton, Trappist monk, theologian and philosopher who was just beginning to explore the commonality of Buddhist and Christian spirituality at the end of his life in 1968. Joseph Campbell, an American literary scholar, drew parallels between traditional myths and religious stories of cultures down through the ages.

Others helping to usher in today's Great Awakening are leaders of the creation spirituality movement, including Matthew Fox, who began his career a Benedictine priest. Father Fox is known for his visionary writings about the Cosmic Christ and his vocal arguments about the need to expand women's role in the Church, and to protect the environment. Now ordained as an Episcopal priest, he ministers to street children in the Bay area of California, and continues to develop his ideas about creation spirituality and lecture worldwide.

We must again bring to mind the Dalai Lama, whose exile from Tibet has only deepened his commitment to non-violence, civil rights and respect for all compassionate religious traditions. Earlier chapters have already mentioned the work of the British theologian Keith Ward, who coined the term Third Age and continues to lay its intellectual groundwork. We also must add John Polkinghorne, Philip Heffner, Arthur Peacocke and others who are advancing the faith and science dialogue.

Now, to insure the dignity and freedom of all people, and to protect the life of the earth, we the people of faith must become join the Third Great Awakening with these enlightened individuals. Let us surrender our pride, our fear and our timidity to embrace the bold work of the Spirit in the Third Great Awakening.

Let us heed the watchwords of transcendence, unity and transformation.

Let us transcend what divides us, the people of faith, and while remaining true to our own traditions, become paradoxically one in our diversity. Let us be transformed into God's loving people; the generation that united to save the diversity of life on earth; who worked for the dignity and freedom of all.

In this transcendent unity, we will find that we have not blurred our individual religious identities. Rather, transformed, we will fulfill them.

Transcendence. Unity. Transformation.

With these watchwords, may we usher in the thousand years of peace.

Notes

Note: Whenever possible, for the reader's convenience in locating these sources, the latest updated reference is provided.

Introduction

1. Reps, Paul, Nyogen Senzake (ed.), *Zen Flesh, Zen Bones: A Collection of Zen and Pre-Zen Writings*, Shambhala Pocket Classics, 1994.

2. Ward, Keith, *A Vision to Pursue: Beyond the Crisis in Christianity*, SCM Press, 1991.

Chapter 1

1. Watts, Alan, *The Way of Zen*, Vintage Books, 1999.

2. A January 1990 "Faith and Science" colloquim at Yale University featured Langdon Gilkey, Ph.D., as keynote speaker discussing the issue of scientific "knowability." In a prepared response to one of Dr. Gilkey's lectures, Leo Hickey, Ph.D., a Yale professor of geology, geophysics and biology, pointed out how Western science is based on the *a priori* assumption that the laws and processes of nature are uniform; that we can explain events universally as outcomes of known causes observed on earth. This belief, he noted, stems from the philosophy of Francis Bacon and John Stuart Mill, and could prove to be the result of the same kind of cultural bias that caused Albert Einstein for years to refuse to believe his own calculations that the universe was expanding.

3. Regarding the teaching of the Cosmic Christ, in "The Creation of the World," a chapter in Volume I of *Christian Dogmatics* (Braaten, Carl E., Jenson, Robert W., eds., Fortress Press, 1984), Phillip Hefner writes of a "correlation between the nature of the world and the nature of the source or creator of the world." And Jaroslav Pelikan, in *Jesus Through the Centuries: His Place in the History of Culture* (Yale University Press, 1987), discusses the early Christian notion of God in Christ reflecting the very structure of the universe. In *The Coming of the Cosmic Christ*, (Harper & Row, 1988), Matthew Fox revisits this ancient teaching in terms of contemporary spirituality; his view of the Cosmic Christ has strongly influenced this book.

4. Ward, Keith, *A Vision to Pursue: Beyond the Crisis in Christianity*, SCM Press, 1993.

5. Monod, Jacques, *Chance and Necessity: An Essay on the Natural Philosophy of Modern Biology*, Knopf, 1971.

Chapter 2

1. Lewis, C.S., *Mere Christianity: Comprising the Case for Christianity, Christian Behaviour, and Beyond Personality*, C.S. Lewis Classics/Touchstone Books, 1996.

Chapter 3

1. Aquinas, St. Thomas, *Summa Theologica*, Christian Classics, 1997.

2. This analysis interprets the vintner's crop in the same sense of Jesus' saying, "The harvest is plentiful, but the laborers are few." [Matthew 9:38]

3. Campbell, Joseph, *The Hero With the Thousand Faces*, Mythos/Princeton University Press, Bolingen Series, 1990.

4. Fox, Matthew, *The Coming of the Cosmic Christ: The Healing of Mother Earth and the Birth of a Global Renaissance*, Harper & Row, 1988.

Chapter 4

1. Pelikan, Jaroslav, *Jesus Through the Centuries: His Place in the History of Culture*, Yale University Press, 1987.

2. Frederiksen, Paula, *From Jesus to the Christ: The Origins of the New Testament Images of Jesus*, Yale University Press, 1990.

Chapter 5

1. Heschel, Abraham Joshua, Dresner, Samuel H. (ed.), *I Asked for Wonder: A Spiritual Anthology*, Crossroad, 1983.

2. Schmitz-Moorman, Karl, Salmon, James F., *Theology of Creation in an Evolutionary World*, The Pilgrim Press, 1997.

Chapter 6

1. Lewis, C.S., *Mere Christianity: Comprising the Case for Christianity, Christian Behaviour, and Beyond Personality*, C.S. Lewis Classics/Touchstone Books, 1996.

2. Clark, Kenneth, *Civilisation*, Harper & Row, 1969.

Chapter 7

1. Eldredge, Niles, *Life in the Balance: Humanity and the Biodiversity Crisis*, Peter N. Nevraumont/Princeton University Press, 1998.

2. Lewis, C.S., *Mere Christianity: Comprising the Case for Christianity, Christian Behaviour, and Beyond Personality*, C.S. Lewis Classics/Touchstone Books, 1996.

3. MacLeish, Archibald, Drabeck, Bernard A., Ellis, Helen E., *Archibald MacLeish: Reflections*, Massachusetts Press, 1986.

Chapter 8

Chernow, Barbara Ann (ed.), Villasi, George A., *The Columbia Encyclopedia, Fifth Edition*, Columbia University Press, 1993.

Chapter 9
Fromm, Erich, *You Shall be as Gods: A Radical Interpretation of the Old Testament and its Tradition*, Henry Holt, 1991.

Chapter 11
1. Fromm, Erich, *You Shall be as Gods: A Radical Interpretation of the Old Testament and its Tradition*, Henry Holt, 1991. (Epigraph altered from male referents to inclusive language.)

2. Lewis, C.S., *Miracles*, Touchstone, 1996.

Chapter 12
1. As discussed in the 1990 Yale Faith and Science colloquium cited in the endnotes for Chapter 1, Heisenberg's uncertainty principle, an outgrowth of quantum mechanics, as well as more recent theories on chaos, have raised doubts as to whether anything in our universe — let alone a phenomenon as complex as human behavior — will ever be absolutely predictable by a human observer.

2. Skinner, Burrhus Frederic, *Beyond Freedom and Dignity*, Alfred A. Knopf, 1971.

3. Ward, Keith, *A Vision to Pursue: Beyond the Crisis in Christianity*, SCM Press, 1993.

3. Lewis, C.S., *Mere Christianity: Comprising the Case for Christianity, Christian Behaviour, and Beyond Personality*, C.S. Lewis Classics/Touchstone Books, 1996.

4. MacLeish, Archibald, Drabeck, Bernard A., Ellis, Helen E., *Archibald MacLeish: Reflections*, Massachusetts Press, 1986.

5. Kushner, *When Bad Things Happen to Good People*, Avon, 1997.

Chapter 13
1. Walls, Jerry L., "Has Hell Frozen Over: Traditional View Still Speaks with Urgency," The Dallas Morning News, July 26, 1997.

2. Boslough, John, *Stephen Hawking's Universe*, William Morrow, 1985.

3. Sullivan, Walter, "Vast Cluster of Galaxies Seen as 'Great Attractor,'" The New York Times, April 28, 1987.

4. Parker Jr., Shafer, "The Best of Times, the End of Times," Vol. 23, *Alberta Report/Western Report*, Dec. 25, 1995.

5. Forer, Eric, Garrety, John A. (eds.), *The Reader's Companion to American History*, Houghton Mifflin, 1991.

Chapter 14

Pelikan, Jaroslav, *Jesus Through the Centuries: His Place in the History of Culture*, Yale University Press, 1987.

Chapter 16

1. Jaroslav Pelikan, in *Jesus Through the Centuries: His Place in the History of Culture* (Yale University Press, 1987), notes Luke's account of Christ's healing of the paralytic (5:17-26). Moved by the stricken man's faith, Jesus declares to him that his sins are forgiven. Then Jesus proceeds to heal the man to prove that he has the power to forgive sin.

2. Pelikan, in *Jesus Through the Centuries*, points out that "the word for 'salvation' — *soteria* in Greek, *salus* in Latin and its derivative languages, *Heil* in German and its cognate languages — mean 'health.'"

Chapter 17

Pelikan, Jaroslav, *Jesus Through the Centuries: His Place in the History of Culture*, Yale University Press, 1987.

Chapter 18

Pelikan, Jaroslav, *Jesus Through the Centuries: His Place in the History of Culture*, Yale University Press, 1987.

Chapter 22

1. Gale Research Inc., *Calendar of Literary Events, Year 1741*, 1994.

2. Walls, Jerry L., "Has Hell Frozen Over: Traditional View Still Speaks With Urgency," The Dallas Morning News, July 26, 1997.

3. Aligheri, Dante; Zappulla, Elio (trans.), *The Inferno*, Pantheon, 1998.

4. Milton, John, *Paradise Lost*, Longman, 1998.

5. Boslough, John, *Stephen Hawking's Universe*, William Morrow, 1985.

6. Sullivan, Walter, "Vast Cluster of Galaxies Seen as 'Great Attractor,' The New York Times, April 28, 1987.

Chapter 24

St. Augustine; Chadwick, Henry (trans.), *Confessions*, Oxford University Press, 1998.

Chapter 25

1. Gregory of Nyssa, *On the Making of Man*, as cited in Pelikan, Jaroslav, *Jesus Through the Centuries: His Place in the History of Culture*, Yale University Press, 1987.

2. Campbell, Joseph, with Moyers, Bill, *The Power of Myth*, Doubleday, 1988.

Chapter 26

1. Groenewold, Sonia C., "Water in the Desert," *The Lutheran*, May 1992.

2. Pennington, M.B., *Centering Prayer: Renewing an Ancient Christian Prayer Form*, Snow Lion Books, 1991.

3. Fromm, Erich, *You Shall be as Gods: A Radical Interpretation of the Old Testament and its Tradition*, Henry Holt, 1991.

4. Watts, Alan, *The Way of Zen*, Vintage Books, 1999.

5. Meier, John P., "Jesus Among the Historians," The New York Times Book Review, Dec. 21, 1986.

Chapter 27
Clendinnen, Inga, *Reading the Holocaust*, Cambridge University Press, 1999.

Chapter 28
1. Gandhi, Mohandas K., *Autobiography: The Story of my Experiments With Truth*, Dover Publications, 1983.

2. Parrinder, Geoffrey (ed.), *World Religion From Ancient History to the Present*, Facts on File, 1971.

3. Ward, Keith, *A Vision to Pursue: Beyond the Crisis in Christianity*, SCM Press, 1991.

4. Campbell, Joseph, with Moyers, Bill, *The Power of Myth*, Doubleday, 1988.

5. Coffin, William Sloane, *The Heart is a Little to the Left: Essays on Public Morality*, Dartmouth College Press, 1999.

6. Fox, Matthew, *The Coming of the Cosmic Christ: The Healing of Mother Earth and the Birth of a Global Renaissance*, Harper & Row, 1988.

Index

I

J

About the Author

A lifelong Christian, Gregory R. Huth has divided much of his adult life between editorial work and community service. As an undergraduate at Yale College in the early 1970s, he was awarded the John Spangler Nicolas Prize for his volunteer efforts on behalf of senior citizens. One lasting contribution from this period is the not-for-profit Sage Advocate Employment Service, co-founded by Mr. Huth, which to the present day has placed tens of thousands of older people in jobs in South Central Connecticut at no charge.

For five years after graduating from Yale, Mr. Huth remained in the New Haven area, joining the VISTA (Volunteers in Service to America) program, organizing a statewide advocacy newspaper for older people called The Connecticut Elder, and co-organizing the New Dimension Theatre Company, a senior citizens troupe.

After returning to Yale University to earn a Master of Public Health degree from the School of Medicine, Mr. Huth renewed his editorial career as a senior editor and associate director of public affairs at CBS Inc. in New York, as publications editor at the Yale University School of Medicine Office of Public Information, and as a managing editor of development for Appleton & Lange, then a Simon & Schuster imprint. He has received two Awards of Excellence in Writing for a Professional Audience from the New England Chapter of the American Medical Writers Association.

In 1997, University Lutheran Ministry at Yale bestowed on Mr. Huth an honorary Melanchthon Fellowship for his 28 years of service to that ministry. The author's current community work includes, along with his wife, Ellen McNally, assisting Tibetan refugees to get settled in the United States. A committed blood donor, in 1999 Mr. Huth received a Bill Savitt-Hall of Fame Award from the Connecticut Chapter of the American Red Cross for having donated 10 gallons of blood.

Today, the author works as president and chief editor of Ivy League Communications Group International.